Just in Time

Also by Robert Creeley

POETRY

For Love • *Words* • *The Charm* • *Pieces*
A Day Book • *Hello: A Journal* • *Later*
Collected Poems: 1945–1975 • *Mirrors*
Memory Gardens • *Selected Poems*
Windows • *Echoes* • *Life & Death*
So There: Poems 1976–83

FICTION

The Gold Diggers • *The Island*
Presences • *Mabel: A Story*
Collected Prose

DRAMA

Listen

ESSAYS

A Quick Graph: Collected Notes & Essays
Was That a Real Poem & Other Essays
Collected Essays
Autobiography
Tales Out of School

ANTHOLOGIES AND SELECTIONS

The Black Mountain Review 1954–1957
New American Story (with Donald M. Allen)
The New Writing in the U.S.A. (with Donald M. Allen)
Selected Writings of Charles Olson
Whitman: Selected Poems
The Essential Burns
Charles Olson, Selected Poems

Robert Creeley

✳

Just in Time

Poems 1984–1994

A New Directions Book

The Preface, "Conversations with Charles Bernstein," was recorded December 11, 1995, for "LINEbreak" (epc.buffalo.edu), produced by Martin Spinelli for the Electronic Poetry Center. Acknowledgments for individual volumes appear on p. 305.

Manufactured in the United States of America
New Directions Books are printed on acid-free paper.
First published as New Directions Paperbook 927 in 2001
Published simultaneously in Canada by Penguin Books Canada Limited
Book design by Erik Rieselbach

Library of Congress Cataloging-in-Publication Data

Creeley, Robert, 1926–
    Just in time : poems, 1984–1994 / Robert Creeley.
    p. cm. – (New Directions paperbook ; 927)
    Includes index.
    Contents: Memory gardens – Windows – Echoes.
    ISBN 0-8112-1487-7 (acid-free paper)
    I. Title
    811'.54–dc21   2001030259

New Directions Books are published for James Laughlin
by New Directions Publishing Corporation,
80 Eighth Avenue, New York, NY 10011

CONTENTS

For Pen, Will, and Hannah

Just in Time

PREFACE: CONVERSATIONS WITH CHARLES BERNSTEIN

PART I: POETRY IN SEARCH OF ITSELF

I'm Charles Bernstein. On today's program: "Poetry In Search of Itself," with Robert Creeley. Robert Creeley's collected essays, poems, and prose are published by the University of California Press. His new collections Echoes *and* Windows *are published by New Directions. Bob, welcome to the program. Today is Pearl Harbor Day, 1995. Do you think of World War II as shaping your poetry in a fundamental way?*

Yes. I think that it did—as the curious climax of the Depression years, in which my generation grew up, then too as an extraordinary "Welcome to the World," which was coincident with leaving home in a final sense, graduating from school and then going on to college. It was a remarkable emphasis upon what the world apparently was content to be. Or, frankly, had come to be.

How did writing poetry, or being a writer...

Well, I don't think that at that age I felt I was either poet or writer. It wasn't that I didn't take myself seriously, but I didn't have any particularizing sense that that was what either I would be or could be. I still thought to be a veterinarian perhaps. And although I had chosen to go to Harvard and had made a commitment to that sense of

1

reading and writing, I hadn't a clue as to how I'd practically undertake either one as a means to make a living or simply to have a life.

You have a poem "Ever Since Hitler," that suggests some sense of your take on that. Would you read that one?

"EVER SINCE HITLER"

Ever since Hitler
or well before that
fact of human appetite
addressed with brutal
indifference others
killed or tortured or ate
the same bodies they
themselves had we ourselves
had plunged into density
of selves all seeming stinking
one no possible way
out of it smiled or cried
or tore at it and died
apparently dead at last
just no other way out.

That seemed the compact of the world. I remember going as, say, an 18-year-old, from Boston, and ending up in Bombay, and just being there in that physical city, and seeing, down by the Burning Ghats, the density, the *physical* density of people. And subsequently over in Calcutta, and also as we went into the circumstance of the war, its scale and brutality … it was really too much … it made "Apocalypse Now" seem rather mild.

The very next poem in Windows—*"Ever Since Hitler" is from* Windows—*is called "Thinking." And it sort of echoes some of those themes, concerns…*

This was published (generously) by Donald Hall in the

Harvard Magazine. It has a certain appropriateness, there-
fore, just as that would be its kind of curious, ironic, reflec-
tive disposition. Although, I've never managed irony with
any confidence, so that it's always finally "serious."

Isn't that the best way to deal with irony?

I guess.

Without confidence. Confident irony is kind of offensive.

Like ironing the clothes.

Like Eliot. Confident irony. It's the opposite of what you want.

I have "unconfident" irony.

THINKING

I've thought of myself
as objective, viz.,
a thing round which
lines could be drawn

or else placed by years, the average
some sixty, say, a relative
number of months, days,
hours and minutes.

I remember thinking of war
and peace and life
for as long as I can remember.
I think we were right.

But it changes, it thinks
it can all go on forever
but it gets older.
What it wants is rest.

I've thought of place
as how long it takes
to get there and of where
it then is.

I've thought of clouds, of water
in long horizontal bodies, or
of love and women and the children
which came after.

Amazing what mind makes
out of its little pictures,
the squiggles and dots,
not to mention the words.

*It seems like suffused violence is something you deal with in a
lot of your work, in many different ways, and in many differ-
ent contexts. So, you know, we could start with Pearl Harbor
Day, but it comes in the mention of words itself, and the vio-
lence of words and of communication. Are there particular
other poets, or ways in which violence is dealt with, that were
useful to you in that way for your own work? Did you feel like
you just had to start from whole cloth?*

Williams was classically useful to me in that way, and
Lawrence to some real extent also. Just that both were
remarkably and engagingly, if that's possible, angry men.
In the sense that Lawrence was both sponsored and pro-
voked by his imagination that the world was a meager
and unresponding place. That people were too often per-
suaded by the most ugly, and curiously, not even despica-
ble … I mean, simply, the most sullen and sodden kinds
of motive. So that the tone in his writing is most often,
not chiding, but a responding anger that people could so
feel and so do things. Williams—I think the predominant
emotion in Williams is one of a kind of repulsion and
anger. And I thought, "Here are my two terrific heroes."
Each had also, without question, an extraordinary inti-

macy, or a "contact" as Williams would say. But they were "classic," to my mind, they were classic Puritans, as I was—who moved in response, rather than in openness or direct accommodation.

Weren't the models that were presented to you, that were available to you at first, in fact, the kinds of poetry that did not deal with...

Initially, I was probably most engaged or persuaded by prose writers. They were, almost without exception, dealing with violence in one form or another. Whether, say, it was Defoe, going back to that time, or particularly the kind of violence active in Dostoevsky, or Kafka, or Gide, for example.

But what's interesting is taking those fiction writers, who deal with struggle and conflict and so on, as the themes of their work. It seems like your work deals with this violence and antagonism within the form, within the structure of writing. And that's why I say it's suffused. I mean, how do you get to that transformation? Reading novelists who write about the subject matter of violence, and yet you've managed—it's not so much that you write about that as a subject, although sometimes you do...

I think it's the curious construction of the ... almost of a "Trojan Horse," it's something ... a cart, or a wagon, or something that ... a conveyance that can carry this particular load in all its implications to whatever point I have in mind, and for whatever point I have in mind or can discover then more actively. I feel as though I don't have "a point" of any remarkable interest, to myself at least. But I do have an activity that's very interesting to me, and that activity, so to speak, is the peculiar recognition of things through the writing itself.

A lot of your work is involved with pulling things apart, and then putting them together, but that "pulling apart" is a very tactile, a very sensual thing. But it also is, you know, kind of a splitting open and rending, or "cleaving," in this marvelous double sense of cleaving, which I think is very much at the heart of it. That both separates, but also it brings back together ... that you work out in the line structure of your work. It is absolutely modulated at every...

I was very attracted to Williams's way of positioning his line breaks. I mean he would "strike into the middle of some trenchant phrase"—whatever, or however, he says it—but the way he so characteristically breaks the line at a point least—not just least expected—but least permitted by the syntactical order. I don't know, I've never known, particularly, what he thought he was doing. I remember my own confusion when I heard a recording of him reading, say, in the early '40's. To recognize that he did not use these linebreaks as any evident pause in his reading at all. Whether he thought of them intelligently or intellectually as being units, I don't know. Whether he was reading syllabically, I could not tell. I knew he put a lot of emphasis—stress—when he read "The tulips/bright tips/sidle and toss"—like that. But the line endings seemed, frankly, the least of his particular concerns. And so I had made a whole procedure out of my reading of him, which served me then very well, in fact, and still in obvious ways does. But it doesn't seem to have been his much at all.

There's a way in which people will doubly read your own line-breaks. Reading it on the page it seems a very formal way of breaking apart the syntax, and at the same time when one hears you read something else happens. There's an emotional valence ... there's a kind of existential quality, a temporal quality, moving from moment to moment, almost in anguish at times in the way the words break, especially recordings from

*the '50s and '60s. That doubleness is very much related. It's a
relation of inside to outside. How do you react to that?*

It makes good sense to me. I recall that there's a surviv-
ing recording of Olson and myself reading. We had gone
to a local place for such recordings outside of Ashville,
N.C., when I was first there at Black Mountain as a visit-
ing teacher. And I don't know whether it was my interest
or his but, in any case, we determined to make a small
record. I think it was mine, because I wanted to send it
to Williams, so that Williams might hear Olson's…

Was this in one of those little recording booths?

Yeah. Exactly.

Like you'd have in a penny arcade?

Yeah, almost. It was a little more sophisticated. It was
an actual studio, but it was that kind. So, a single small
record. And we sent it to Williams, and it was useful. He
could therefore hear what Olson's line was proposing to
do, because here now was Olson literally reading it. And
he was an extraordinary reader.

*I love the term "record," as we now have here very sophisti-
cated equipment. The idea of making a record is very much
like making a mark. The linebreaks are a very important part
of the visual mark, and a very important part of the acoustic
mark, of your work. Are you conscious of that in reading? I
mean Williams, when one hears him read, we don't hear the
breaks, as so often is remarked, there's not space in there. But
you read the breaks.*

I read the breaks. To me, like percussive or contrapuntal
agencies, they give me a chance to get a syncopation into
the classic emptiness: "it sits out there / edge of / hierarchic

rooftop/it…" I mean it gives me, not drumming precisely, but it's a rhythm of that character. "It marks with acid fine edge/of apparent difference/It is there/here here that sky/so up and up/and where…," you know. It's also an agency for a lot of half-rhyming or accidental echoing, that I really enjoy. It's also sort of like water sloshing in a pan, not just like that—but that would be an apt analogy. Lapping at the edges.

Which is also a play between inside and outside, that works both to describe the form of the poem and the content. Also, I think it has to do again with where the violence is. The violence is within yourself. It's not just in somebody else, it's not always directed outside…

No. Would that it were, would that it would also settle down and forget it. I wrote a poem called "Anger" years ago, which is probably as accurate a sense of it as I ever managed. And then too, in the early stories, *The Gold Diggers,* it's there that the anger is very explicit. It's clear in the one novel I wrote—*The Island*—it's a complicated, impacted, It isn't despair. I don't think I ever felt significant despair, but I certainly felt anger.

Can you read "What"?

Yeah.

Or, as they would say in England, "Can you read, what?"

I could read "What."

You have all those in your catalogue of poems, like "What," "It." I was going to ask you what "it" meant in the poem you read before. What is "it"?

WHAT

What had one thought the
outside was but place all
evident surface and each
supposed perspect touched
texture all the wet implicit
world was adamant edge of
limit responsive if indifferent
and changing (one thought) in-
side its own evident kind one
banged upon abstract insens-
itive else echoed in passing
was it the movement one's own?

*Your work often plays off the lyric poem, the solitary self-express-
ing. It/his/your/my failings. But overpowering this expressive
individual is a sense of company, and you use the word "com-
pany," you have a poem called "Company," that maybe you'll
read in a second, but "company" in the work of poetry. How is
your work affected or influenced by this company?*

Well, it's not a … it's not necessarily a team, although it
probably would like to be…

*It's true that your use of the word "company" is always and for-
ever never like a corporation. It's never that sense of company.*

If you read it, you recognize that it's not simply name-
dropping—not at all—it's locating "the company." I re-
member one of our friends here had shown me a curious
page or two from a journal of John Cheever's that was
being published by the *Paris Review*. And Cheever is re-
membering my coming to Briarcliffe, to read. And it
speaks about my hair. He is seemingly intrigued by my
preoccupation with my hair, and my hands constantly
running through it, etc. But, more to the point, he says,
"he talks so much about the people that he knows … not
only that he likes them obviously, he talks about Leslie

Fiedler, he talks about X, Y, or Z as though he is proud of them." Not that he knows them simply, but that he's proud of them. And that sense of a company, almost like "The Musicians of Bremen," I really love that sense. You know, that one could drink the ocean, another could live in the fiery furnaces, one could take seven league strides. I love that sense of a company. And I felt that way extraordinarily with friends at that time. I guess I had little "company," in one sense, in poetry at first, and then terrifically, I had a lot of company. Whatever its occasion or literary value, it was great.

It has another effect, as a reader, in that for me, the work provides company. One could be very moved by a lyric poem and the feelings the individual is expressing or the beauty of the expression. But this is different. There is something about reading your work which seems to provide company.

That's great! My work is done.

I don't think I'm alone in that. It's a formal experience of the work, and the way in which one enters into it, I think.

I was moved, as they say, in England recently at some wildly and pleasantly particular occasion, somewhere way out on the edge on the way to Cornwall. I'd taken a train across the country, from Durham actually, all the way across to Reading, and then to Exeter, and then had gone from Exeter, driven by car another hour or so, down to Torrington, and was now to read. The point was, afterwards, someone said it was just as though one were sitting in one's living room or something. And I thought, that's precisely the place I'd love to have it all be. I love that sense of "Come closer and I'll tell you a story…"

And even as you say "living room," it takes on a literal sense. Could you read "The Company?"

Yeah. This was written, one might note, for what I presumed would be a company of the young...

I can't imagine the Signet Society...

I thought I knew a little of the Signet Society, having—as you had—gone to Harvard, but I didn't. Seymour Lawrence, I believe, was the only friend ever in it. But it was much more august, we realized, than the *Advocate* or any of the more public clubs, like the *Lampoon* or whatever. But in any case, I was invited to be the poet, I think they paid some money and I got a meal, and so on and so forth. So I went very innocently. I remember everything on my body was rented, except my underwear, literally.

This was 1985. I can't imagine going totally innocently in 1985...

My shoes were rented, my tie, my shirt, my pants. It was formal dress.

Oh, it was formal dress. I should emphasize to the radio listeners that you are in informal dress, but with a full head of hair here today...

Thank you. In any case, I had expected that this would be an occasion primarily for the undergraduates who were members of the society. Not so. There was a reception prior to it, in which we were told that they were raising something like ... they were raising money for the society. I think the proposed goal was $2 million. I was thinking of some of our usefully humble enterprises here in Buffalo. Theirs was to take literary people to lunch! Not to publish anything, but to literally provide food and entertainment for the visitor and themselves. So anyhow, all the proceedings were in Latin.

In Latin?

In Latin.

How's your Latin?

Not too good. But anyhow, this poem was written, as I
say, for the imagination—my imagination—of the young.
Trying to tell them, in a funny sense, what it had been like
to be a student at Harvard in the early '40's.

THE COMPANY

for the Signet Society, April 11, 1985

Backward—as if retentive.
"The child is father to the man"
or some such echo of device,
a parallel of use and circumstance.

Scale become implication.
Place, postcard determinant—
only because someone sent it.
Relations—best if convenient.

"Out of all this emptiness
something must come…" Concomitant
with the insistent banality, small, still
face in mirror looks simply vacant.

Hence blather, disjunct, incessant
indecision, moving along on
road to next town where what waited
was great expectations again, empty plate.

So there they were, expectably ambivalent,
given the Second World War
"to one who has been long in city pent,"
trying to make sense of it.

We—*morituri*—blasted from classic
humanistic *noblesse oblige,* all the garbage

12

of either so-called side, hung on
to what we thought we had, an existential

raison d'être like a pea
some faded princess tries to sleep on,
and when that was expectably soon gone,
we left. We walked away.

Recorders ages hence will look for us
not only in books, one hopes, nor only under rocks
but in some common places of feeling,
small enough—but isn't the human

just that echoing, resonant edge
of what it knows it knows,
takes heart in remembering
only the good times, yet

can't forget whatever it was,
comes here again, fearing this
is the last day, this is the last,
the last, the last.

Robert Creeley reading "The Company" from Windows. *You
mentioned a few times in the last comments that you made the
word "authority." The kind of false authority of the poets that
you were rejecting ... different kinds of authority. Does poetry
have authority? Do poets have authority?*

I was thinking in a sense that Duncan uses from Blake—
"The authors are in eternity." So that's a sense of authori-
ty. But the authority one basically deals with socially or
politically is the authority that is implicit in "it is written."
It's a duly stamped and signed by appropriate persons'
authority. "We are the authority. We can authorize this.
You can't."

*It seems like also so much of your work is a backing away
from, or questioning, or intense anxiety in the face of aspects
of authority.*

13

Ezra Pound used to emphasize that there was a time in critical writing, reviewing—he uses it with reference to the *Times Literary Supplement*—when articles were not signed. Not because they were, you know, cheap shots and the writers did not want to stand up for their statements, but because it was thought too egocentric to want one's name to be attached. I certainly love Hart Crane's "I dreamt that all men dropped their names and sang," you know, "struck free and holy in one name always." Which is certainly a large, vatic, and obviously sentimental desire, but I would comfortably share it with him. I would love to see again a company, wherein one could sing with everybody without having a peculiar argument for significant singularity. And yet I know when younger, I was certainly a very competitive poet. Ruthlessly so, in many cases. I was looking at the second volume of Charles Bukowski's letters, certainly a loner if there ever was one, and I mean after years of singling me out as the only poet he really wants to, you know, not so much get, but who he feels is worthy of his absolute anger and attack. I remember...

Target.

Yeah, the "target." When he first came to New York, St. Mark's it was actually, some friend there said, "The only poet he mentioned all night long, Bob, was you. And he just wanted to say how much he disliked you." Anyhow, in his later letters, which are very sweet and funny often, he suddenly says something to the effect, "You know Creeley should be permitted his tantrums. He has sort of earned them. After all, he is intelligent." I thought, God, that's such a peculiar reassurance coming from Charles Bukowski! We recognized each other. It wasn't simply that he was, you know, a "barfly," etc. But the tenacity and the curious authority he managed to make for his own acts was very, very impressive.

14

FIRST LOVE

This is a terrifying poem of my young manhood...

Oh your face is there a mirror days
weeks we lived those other places in
all that ridiculous waste the young we
wanted not to be walked endless streets
in novels read about life went home at
night to sleep in tentative houses left
one another somewhere now unclear no per-
sons really left but for paper a child or
two or three and whatever physical events
were carved then on that tree like initials
a heart a face of quiet blood and somehow
you kept saying and saying an unending pain.

I'm Charles Bernstein. On today's program: "Poetry On the Line" with Robert Creeley. Robert Creeley's Selected Poems *has just been published by the University of California Press,* Windows *and* Echoes *are new from New Directions. He teaches in the Poetics Program at the State University of New York at Buffalo. Bob, two of the poets you often invoke—Pound and Olson—wrote epic poems, poems encompassing history, poems incorporating political and cultural documents. But your own poems seem very much the opposite of that.*

I remember having one called "Epic." "Leave some room / for my epic." That's the poem. I could never get rolling on an epic scale, so to speak.

Why is it that you are drawn, as models, to these...

Well, they're good people to hang out with. Like, "speak to the man, child." They gave me a necessary confidence, so to speak.

Well, measure is something you often write about, and think about, and your sense of measure seems anti-epic. Although I wouldn't say minimal, as it might be described.

Like Laurel and Hardy. I was fascinated by their abilities, both to think "the" world, or a ... no, "the world" such as I also variously knew it, and to find a way of, not compacting it or compounding it, but—not of representing it—but of thus using it as though they, not took control of it, but could act in all of its various terms. And were very stylish, and very—despite the obvious horrors of some of the circumstances, nonetheless were, as poets, great.

But what about your poems' measure? What do your poems measure?

I guess that one echo might be Blake's sense of "to see the world in a grain of sand," the scale really in Herrick's poems, in Zukofsky's in some ways, despite that Zukofsky wrote a longer poem indeed. Nonetheless, his focus curiously feels very akin to mine. I don't know. I was a piece worker. I liked the sense of, not so much "poem poem poem," but I liked the sense of having these various things, or facets, or reflections. All of which could be started over and over. Francesco Clemente made this charming remark, he said, "Unlike the painter's line, the poet gets the chance to start his or her line new everytime."

But what's the prosody of that? I mean Zukofsky always talks about music, of his poetry, and your prosody seems an extension of a musical and prosodic idea that relates to Zukofsky.

I love the way it refracts and sounds in the head. That, to me, was the fascination of poetry early on, its unexpected resonance. I remember one time, with Robert Duncan, we were thinking particularly about how long something could be … how long it would sound after it was spoken. Not simply how long it would hang in the air, but if one said "Boo" as the opening sound, let's say, how many other syllables of sound, or units of sound, could one then add, and still have "Boo" resonate and come back "true."

There's something uncanny in your work, which I'd say is like the sound of thinking. Sometimes I hear thinking sounded, in the way that, in Walden, *Thoreau talks about sounding the bottom of Walden Pond to get its shape, but also the sound coming in time. I'm thinking of the poem "Whatever."*

Right.

WHATEVER

Whatever's
to be
thought
of thinking
thinking's
thought of
it still
thinks
it thinks
to know
itself so
thought.

.

Thought so
itself know to
thinks it
thinks still it
of thought
thinking's
thinking
of thought
be to
whatever's.

I love the word "whatever." Really the key to that poem
is simply that terrific word "whatever," which is a very
curious word. To have "what" and "ever" thus together!

*I'm thinking of loops, echoes, measures. Your poems have been
set, in a lot of different ways. You set them yourself in a perfor-
mance situation. But you had an extraordinary series of collab-
orations with visual artists. One I'm thinking of right now is
Cletus Johnson, who actually put your poems in theaters, and
also set them around as loops, as circles. These are interesting
performance spaces. Could you talk about the theaters and the
loops? And maybe read some?*

Yes. Cletus worked for a time with Louise Nevelson, but he's not interested in that particular sort of scale, but he is interested in that particular making of a theatrical space. A shadow box. There are aspects of Cornell, for example. Collaging, he loves.

They're more model-size theaters rather than something you can actually walk into.

Exactly. For a long time he concentrated on what one wants to call "architectural detail." And he very rarely used words. Usually at most a name. So these works had a curious classic elegance. They were really interesting, and they were brilliant, singular art. But a few years ago he was interested to do something that would involve language in some way, and he was thinking of marquees on theaters and words going around on loops of lights, and of bills ... theater bills. Things of that sort. He also wanted something, if possible, that could be continuous. Such as a string of lights announcing something. So that was the scale. That was the context, more accurately, and the scale had to be ... necessarily had to be ... modest. Simply that the scale of the piece would not let one, you know, go on and on and on. A quatrain was an ideal size. Or a couplet. I think we both wanted something that could go round and round. And I can remember one of the very first we did was one called "Fat Fate."

Be at That this
Come as If when
Stay or Soon then
Ever happen It will

And it would go round and around. And I'd say, "What the heck is that saying?" It's—I don't know what it's saying. I mean I do know what it's saying in my own interests, but I don't know what it's saying to other people particularly. But I love it. "Be at," that is, be present to "that this," or the fact you actually were there in time and space. "Come as If when / Stay or Soon then / Ever happen It will."

It's also a series of double stress beats.

Yeah, it's double stress beats, and it's also…

And it also goes continuously. It doesn't stop. And everything links from the two beats to the next two beats.

Sometimes—there were several in the whole sequence—Cletus would say, "I have this little hand that I want to use in a piece. Can you write something with 'hand' in it?" I mean, the great pleasure in doing these things was just that.

Talk about doing piecework!

Yeah, exactly. He was living … he lives happily … he has a studio just south of Buffalo down in Ellington. So we'd have this charming ride down to see what Cletus was up to. He lives in an old classic feedstore, a converted feedstore.

You like to work that way, when someone gives you a project or something to do.

Yeah. I love "things to do today" or, you know, "Bob, can you do something…"

Can you write something with "hand," Bob?

Yeah. It's called "Here."

Outstretched innocence
Implacable distance
Lend me a hand
See if it reaches

I remember writing that on the seat of the jeep we were in.

Can you loop that around one more time?

Outstretched innocence
Implacable distance
Lend me a hand
See if it reaches

I can lend you a Coke. But my hands are all tied up.

One other of these, and … this was an early one, I re-
member. Again, the very obvious loop of just parallel
syntax.

TIME

Of right Of wrong Of up Of down
Of who Of how Of when Of one
Of then Of if Of in Of out
Of field Of friend Of it Of now

*And there's another one like this that I like very much called
"Just In Time." Which has a sense, also, of the measure of time
as it passes. As a loop.*

Right. Absolutely. It's for Anne Waldman, actually.

JUST IN TIME

Over the unwritten
and under the written

and under and over
and in back and in front of
or up or down or in
or in place of, of not,
of this and this, of
all that is, of it.

It's almost hard to imagine that you could have a poem composed of such common words, such simple words. I mean, "unwritten" and "written," are three and two syllables. Much of the rest is made up of one syllable words: "of," "place," and "Just In Time" itself.

I think of "thee," "my country 'tis of thee."

A cliché or an everyday expression.

Yeah.

"You've come just in time." "Just in time/I found you…" — the song.

I love it. "Just In Time." Charlie Parker.

How do you make a poem of such basic words?

I don't know. It's a curious answer. If something provokes … no magical sense, but something provokes a premise or a case. Not even "this is it," but what else can be if this is it. What's the consequence of this being it, or what is the imagination of the "it" that is thus 'this.' And so on and so forth. So it begins, "Over the unwritten." I was thinking of something … that something hasn't been "unwritten," and something is overwritten, but what does that constitute? What does that prove to be? And I was thinking of the "unwritten" law, you know. That over and above that something else, "and under the written," something is inherent, or something is given a part of, obviously, from that which is simply "written." The "under" underwrites it. "And under and over/and in back and in front of," all the positional ways we have of qualifying things for our purposes. "Or in place of…" begins to now move into another sense of "how am I going to get out of this?" "Of not," in other words, a sense that there is a whole place found in saying that it isn't here, you know.

Making a poem up of words like "place" and "not" and "down" and "in" and "or" is very different than a kind of diction, of subject matter, that I associate with a conventional kind of poetry. You know, probably the kind of poetry you read when you were growing up, and even the poetry of Pound and Olson that you are talking about. Using these simple words, these ordinary words. You seem to have a constant desire to return to the ordinary, to the everyday, to the vernacular, to what you sometimes refer to as the "common place," or "the commons." But the commons of language.

Our mother, thinking of my sister Helen and myself, I don't think she had any conscious sense of constraining us in this way, or intending to, but somehow in our family there was a great … there was, apparently, a great fear of putting on airs, or of representing oneself other than particularly in one's own imagination, or understanding, of who or what one was. So it wasn't some irritable question of "high-falutin'"—that curiously wasn't really the emphasis. But it was an absolute, almost didactic, fear of misrepresentation, of misrepresenting the terms. Either my mother got it through through her activity, her practice as a nurse. The dilemmas of representing things to the patients. Whatever. Possibly in relation to herself, being a single parent. Possibly in relation to us, and her parents were with us as well. But, in any case, there was a sense of dogged necessity to say things, to "tell it like is," also compounded with the fact that she was immensely discreet. She could talk very openly and comfortably about the physical body, because of being a nurse. But emotional terms were much more complicated for her, and she was quite diffident about her own feelings.

Well, I can understand a sense of New England economy.

Yeah.

Concreteness...

Well, there were a lot of people in New England, certainly, who didn't talk in this way at all, you know. I mean, this certainly isn't, for instance, Robert Frost.

Yeah. That's the highly rhetorical "other."

It does echo in particular poets, such as Edwin Arlington Robinson. That "down which the blind are driven," the classic anthology poem of his, "Eros Tyrranos." The way the words meld with this almost tinkly piano-like rhythm, but the end of the poem is so flat, but so unrhetorical in its emphasis. Another great poem of his is "Man Against the Sky," which, again, is so determinedly flat, not in emotion but "flat" in terms of language.

But what's great about "Just In Time" is that it is impossible for someone to say.

No.

What's great about this poem is that it's not sayable, so that you get from something that's concrete and direct, into something that's impossible. You get from something in which you're trying to avoid abstraction, when you're talking about your mother, into something that's highly abstract.

Absolutely abstract.

It's a kind of alchemy.

Exactly. For example, in our family there were occasions when we would be, necessarily and usefully, talking with a psychiatrist. Some common family dilemma. All of us. And I recall the psychiatrist, very benign, would almost always remark that my language was very abstract. I wish I had had more time to talk to him! I didn't know whether he meant that he found me hard to understand, or that it was hard to take in what I was saying and to give it a concrete reference or base.

There's a double sense of "abstract," of course, like an "abstraction." Like "abstracting juices," so that it becomes concentrated.

Yeah.

Can you read "Here"?

Yeah.

HERE

In other
words opaque
disposition intended
for no one's interest
or determination
forgotten ever
increased but
inflexible and
left afterwards.

It's like "I don't want to bother anybody." This is a poem which will offend no one. It will engage no one.

Robert Creeley reading "Here" from Windows. *So whenever "here," there is also an echo, and in every echo a "here." And there's also a kind of emptiness in an echo, as it resonates from one to the other. And it's as if that time — the measure — in this poem, and others of yours, slows everything down. And it's that slowing down that's also...*

Do you remember that sense of ... I think it was T. S. Eliot. The classic wave that breaks ... he uses it as his sense of time, that moment, that instant, the edge before the wave curls. Which is an impending current of the future that's going to break into those long, sort of calming ripples and rupples. Ruffles, or whatever. All that "what's past," etc., etc.

So that echoes sound echoes? Are they waves?

Yeah. They're waves. It's a wave form.

You have many poems called "Echo." Or anyways, some poems called "Echo."

Many poems called "Echo." For a long time I had a lot of poems called "Song." Lots of poems called "Here." As opposed to "there." Some poems called "There."

But it's not Echo, like Narcissus.

No. Or it's not that echo. I was tempted to use as a model, "Little Sir Echo, how do you do ... Hello, 'hello' ..." You know that funny song. But it really isn't that kind either. But it is an "echo." It's that sense of "echo" as the classic Echo, who both mocks and echoes, or resonates, whatever it was that was there.

For me, your echoes are not the echoes of a narcissist, who gets an echo back of herself or himself. Sees her or his own image.

27

It's more like sonograms.

Yeah. It is like a literal echo, like "hello," but it's more like Keats' echo, or that sense of "forlorn, the very word is like a...," you know...

With sonograms, one's sending out soundwaves and they bounce back, and that gives you the image.

The shape...

The sound image. Would you read "Echo: For J.L.?"

Yeah, "J.L." was an old friend here for years. John Logan. A fellow poet here in Buffalo.

ECHO

Outside the
trees
make limit of
simple

sight. The
weather is
a grey, cold on
the

skin. It feels
itself
as if a place it
couldn't

ever get to
had been at
last
entered.

One of my favorite sequences of yours in recent years is called

"Helsinki Window." Could you talk a little about that poem? The form, the shape of it?

Yeah.

They look like windows, don't they?

Yeah. It was a window. We had rented—or rather, it had been provided for us—an apartment with a modest rent in a very good-natured circumstance. It was an easy walk into the center of the city of Helsinki. And it was actually the apartment of the family whose father is now the president of Finland, Martti Ahtisaari. And so it had this room. Thinking of things common, it was remarkably so, given that he was then Finland's representative at the United Nations. And I was working—while he was working at the United Nations—I was working in his very modest study.

And the one window looked out on the central courtyard. It was this great sort of apartment block interior where people would, you know, park occasionally. And basically it was just a space to put out the garbage bins and what not. So that window became my intimate companion and reference, day and night. I could sort of peek out at the neighbors variously, but I could also see the sky. It was up high enough to see out over the roofs to the open sky of the city. Once I had got sort of settled into it, "Helsinki Window," at the window, I didn't feel literally like a 'shut-in,' but I was certainly occupying that window much as, say, someone constrained to be in that room might do as well. And it was also interesting, for me, the sequence, because this is the first time for my use of this form, so-called, this particular 12-line stanza or whatever to call it. Almost like a sonnet in its determined compacting. "Helsinki Window" was the most sustained and particularizing use of this 12-line stanza or form.

At first I had thought of it as a series of singular poems.

I mean, all these poems had, in fact, titles. But then, they began to be the "window," began to be the locating and bonding element, so to speak, throughout.

They're long, relatively long, lines for you too ...

Yeah. They're very impacted. I mean, I had taken a sense of it from Olson, for example. Certainly his later poems. Also from Jack Clark. I'm very interested in this kind of "everything turned in." And also the syntactical resolution delayed until the very close of the poem. Then it can almost start over again.

It loops as well.

Nothing is permitted to quite end, or stop, until the final word of the poem. And it's not particularly dramatic, although it resolves syntactically at that point. But there's no surprise, remarkably. The first one, for example, is again literal. One is looking out a window, and thus entering a more opening space.

Go out into brightened
space out there the fainter
yellowish place it
makes for eye to enter out
to greyed penumbra all the
way to thoughtful searching
sight of all beyond that
solid red both brick and seeming
metal roof or higher black
beyond the genial slope I
look at daily house top on
my own way up to heaven.

      •

Same roof, light's gone
down back of it, behind
the crying end of day, "I

need something to do," it's
been again those other
things, what's out there,
sodden edge of sea's
bay, city's graveyard, park
deserted, flattened aspect,
leaves gone colored fall
to sidewalk, street, the end
of all these days but
still this regal light.

The light in Finland was just mind-blowing, whether it
was in the diminution of it towards the center of the year,
in the winter. But, equally, this vatic light that would
then come back at the edge of summer.

Then there were two other places in the poem that I
love. One part was first called "Jiménez's Elegiacs." I was
at a reading in Trento with some really terrific, old-time
Italian poet about my age, and I was sitting there with a
friend, who said afterward—she was a classic Spaniard—
she said, "Jiménez's elegiacs…" Meaning he's just trying
to do the poet Juan Ramon Jiménez's elegiacs. So this
was my attempt to do "Jiménez's elegiacs."

He was at the edge of this
reflective echo the words blown
back in air a bubble of suddenly
apparent person who walked to
sit down by the familiar brook and
thought about his fading life
all "fading life" in tremulous airy
perspect saw it hover in the surface
of that moving darkness at the edge
of sun's passing water's sudden depth
his own hand's knotted surface the
sounding in himself of some other.

Then one has a curious parody of Frost. And also, I
wanted a focus that moved from the self to concerns,

literally, outside. This is simply looking out the same
window. At a given time—1:45 P.M.

One forty five afternoon red
car parked left hand side
of street no distinguishing
feature still wet day a bicycle
across the way a green door—
way with arched upper window
a backyard edge of back wall
to enclosed alley low down small
windows and two other cars green
and blue parked too and miles
and more miles still to go.

Robert Creeley, reading from Windows.

Memory Gardens

Well, while I'm here I'll
            do the work—
and what's the work?
        To ease the pain of living.
Everything else, drunken
            dumbshow.

—Allen Ginsberg,
                                "Memory Gardens"

One

HEAVEN KNOWS

Seemingly never until one's dead
is there possible measure —

but of what then or for what
other than the same plagues

attended the living with misunderstanding
and wanted a compromise as pledge

one could care for any of them
heaven knows, if that's where one goes.

FORTY

The forthright, good-natured faith
of man hung on crane up

forty stories with roof scaffolding
burning below him forty feet,

good warm face, black hair,
confidence. He said, when

the firemen appeared, he said
I'm glad to see you,

glad not to be there alone.
How old? Thirty, thirty-five?

He has friends to believe in,
those who love him.

OUT

Within pitiless
indifference
things left
out.

NEW ENGLAND

Work, Christian, work!
Love's labors before you go
carrying lights like the
stars are all out and
tonight is the night.

TOO LATE

You tried to answer the questions attractively,
your name, your particular interests,

what you hoped life would prove,
what you owned and had with you,

your so-called billfold an umbilical,
useless, to the sack you'd carried

all your sad life, all your vulnerability,
but couldn't hide, couldn't now say,

brown hair, brown eyes, steady,
I think I love you.

ROOM

Quick stutters of incidental
passage going back

and forth, quick
breaks of pattern, slices

of the meat, two
rotten tomatoes, an incidental

snowstorm, death, a girl
that looks like you later

than these leaves of
grass, trees, birds, under

water, empty passage-
way, and no way back.

HOTEL

It isn't in the world of
fragile relationships

or memories, nothing
you could have brought with you.

It's snowing in Toronto.
It's four-thirty, a winter evening,

and the tv looks like a faded
hailstorm. The people

you know are down the hall,
maybe, but you're tired,

you're alone, and that's happy.
Give up and lie down.

ECHO

Pushing out from
this insistent

time makes
all of it

empty, again
memory.

EARTH

And as the world is flat or round
out over those difficult dispositions

of actual water, actual earth,
each thing invariable, specific,

I think no rock's hardness,
call on none to gainsay me,

be only here as and forever
each and every thing is.

DOGS

I've trained them
to come,

to go away again,
to sit, to stand,

to wait
on command,

or I'd like to
be the master who

tells them all
they can't do.

VISION

Think of the size of it,
so big, if you could remember
what it was or where.

RELIGION

Gods one would have
hauled out like props
to shore up the invented
inside-out proposals

of worlds equally like shams
back of a shabby curtain
only let in the duped,
the dumbly despairing.

41

So flutter the dead
back of the scene
and along with them
the possibly still living.

THE ROCK

Shaking hands again
from place of age,
out to the one

is walking down
the garden path
to be as all reunited.

THANKSGIVING'S DONE

All leaves gone, yellow
light with low sun,

branches edged
in sharpened outline

against far-up pale sky.
Nights with their blackness

and myriad stars, colder
now as these days go by.

GO

Push that little
thing up and the
other right down.
It'll work.

MAIN AND MERRIMAC

"It just plain
hurts to work—"
Christ holds
up hands in
mock despair
concrete bright
sun with faint
first green of
leaves this morn-
ing's gone to
spring's first day.

FOR PEN

Lady moon
light white
flowers open
in sweet silence.

FOR J.D.

Seeing is believing —
times such things
alter all one
had known.

These times, places,
old, echoing
clothes, hands — tools,
almost walking.

Your heart *as big as all outdoors...*
where tree grows,
gate was
waiting.

ALWAYS

Sweet sister Mary's gone
away. Time fades on and on.

The morning was so bright, so clear
blurs in the eye, fades also.

Time tells what after all.
It's always now, always here.

EDGE

Edge of place
put on between

its proposed
place in

time
and space.

MASSACHUSETTS MAY

Month one was born in
particular emphasis
as year comes round
again. Laconic, diverse

sweet May of my boyhood,
as the Memorial Day Parade
marches through those memories.
Or else the hum and laze

of summer's sweet patterns,
dragonflies, grasshoppers,
ladyslippers, and ponds—
School's end. Summer's song.

MEMORIES

Hello, duck,
in yellow

cloth stuffed from
inside out,

little
pillow.

ECHO

Back in time
for supper
when the lights

Two

WALL

I've looked at this wall
for months, bricks
faded, chipped, edge of roof

fixed with icicles
like teeth,
arch of window

opposite, blistered
white paint, a trim
of grey blue.

Specific limit—
of what? A shell
of house, no one's home,

tenuous,
damp emptiness
under a leaky roof.

Careless of what else,
wall so close,
insistent,

to my own—
can push
with eye, thinking

where one can't go,
those crushed
in so-called blackness,

despair. This easy
admission's
no place walls

can echo,
real or unreal.
They sit between

inside and out—
like in school, years ago,
we saw *Wall*, heard

Wall say, "Thus have I,
Wall, my part discharged so;/
And, being done,

thus Wall away doth go"—
Clouds overhead, patch of
shifting blue sky. Faint sun.

I'LL WIN

I'll win the way
I always do
by being gone
when they come.

When they look, they'll see
nothing of me
and where I am
they'll not know.

This, I thought, is my way
and right or wrong
it's me. Being dead, then,
I'll have won completely.

EATS

Self-shrinking focus
mode of deployment
of people met in casual
engagement, social—

Not the man I am
or even was, have constructed
some pattern, place
will be as all.

Bored, shrink into
isolated fading
out of gross, comfortable
contact, hence *out to lunch.*

FOR THE NEW YEAR

Rid forever of *them* and *me,*
the ridiculous small places
of the patient hates, the meager

agreement of unequal people—
at last all subject to
hunger, despair, a common grief.

BOOKCASE

One cannot offer
to emptiness

more than regret. The persons
no longer are there,

their presence become
a resonance, something

inside. Postcard—
"still more to have…

"of talking to you"—
found in book

in this chaos—
dead five years.

BABY DISASTER

Blurred headlights of the cars out there
war of the worlds or something,
ideas of it all like dropped change,
trying to find it on the sidewalk at night.

Nothing doing anymore, grown up, moved out,
piddling little's going to come of it,
all you put in the bank or spent
you didn't want to, wanted to keep it all.

Walk on by, baby disaster.
Sad for us all finally, totally,
going down like in Sargasso Sea
of everything we ever thought to.

SOUND

Shuddering racket of
air conditioner's colder

than imagined winter,
standing lonely,

constancy's not
only love's,

not such faith
in mere faithfulness—

sullen sound.

FOR J.D. (2)

Pass on by, love,
wait by that garden gate.
Swing on, up
on heaven's gate.

The confounding, confronted
pictures of world
brought to signs
of its insistent self

are here in all colors, sizes—
a heart as big as all outdoors,
a weather of spaces,
intervals between silences.

PICTURE

for D.L.

Great giggles,
chunky lumps,
packed flesh,
good nature—

like an apple,
a pear, an immaculate
strawberry, a
particular pomegranate.

And that's the way you saw me, love?
Just so.
Was there nothing else struck you?
No.

FOUR FOR JOHN DALEY

MOTHER'S THINGS

I wanted approval,
carrying with me
things of my mother's
beyond their use to me—

worn-out clock,
her small green lock box,
father's engraved brass plate
for printing calling cards—

such size of her still
calls out to me
with that silently
expressive will.

ECHO

Lonely in
no one
to hold it with—

the responsible
caring
for those one's known.

LEAVING

My eye teared,
lump in throat—
I was going
away from here

and everything that
had come with me
first was waiting
again to be taken.

All the times
I'd looked, held,
handled that or this
reminded me

no fairness, justice,
in life, not
that can stand
with those abandoned.

BUFFALO AFTERNOON

Greyed board fence
past brown open door,
overhead weather's
early summer's.

The chairs sit various,
what's left, the
emptiness, this
curious waiting to go.

I look up to eyes
of Willy's battered
plastic horse, a dog
for its face.

All here,
even in the absence
as if all were
so placed in vacant space.

FORT WILLIAM HENRY / PEMAQUID

Squat round stone tower
o'erlooks the quiet water.

Might in olden days here
had literally accomplished power

as they must have hauled the rocks
from the coves adjacent

to defend their rights
in this abstract place

of mind and far waters
they'd come all the way over

to where presently small son paddles,
flops on bottom in sea's puddle.

NOTHING

Ant pushes across rock face.
No sign of age there

nor in the outstretched water
looks like forever.

Dried seaweed, this ground-down sand,
or the sky where sun's reached peak

and day moves to end—
still nothing done, enough said.

FOR TED BERRIGAN

After, size of place
you'd filled
in suddenly emptied
world all too apparent

and as if New England
shrank, grew physically
smaller like Connecticut,
Vermont—all the little

things otherwise unattended
so made real by you,
things to do today,
left empty, waiting

sadly for no one
will come again now.
It's all moved inside,
all that dear world

in mind for forever,
as long as one walks
and talks here,
thinking of you.

HOTEL SCHRIEDER, HEIDELBERG

Offed tv screen's
reflection room
across with gauze
draped window see
silent weeping face
Marcel Marceau from
balcony seat was memory's
Paris early fifties how
was where and when
with whom we
sat there, watching?

"ICH BIN…"

Ich Bin
2 Öl-tank

yellow squat
by railroad

shed train's
zapped past

round peculiar
empty small

town's ownership
fields' flat

production towered
by obsolescent hill-

side memory echoing
old worn-out castle.

APRÈS ANDERS

HAHA

In her hair the
moon, with
the moon, wakes water—

balloon hauls her
into the blue. She

fängt, she
in the woods
faints, finds, fakes

fire, high in
Erlen, oil, Earl—

like a *Luftschiffern,*
tails of high clouds up
there, one says.

KAPUT KASPER'S LATE LOVE

I was
"kaput Kasper"
in *Fensterfrost,*

window shade auntie,
mother's faltering bundle.
Blood flecks on some
wind flint horizon.

I knew my swollen loaf,
Lauf, like, out, *aus*
es floats, it *flötete.*

Sie sagte, said
the night stuck
two eyes in her heart (head).

I *griff,* grabbed, griped,
in the empty holes, held
on to holes

unter der Stirn,
under stars, the stars
in the sky tonight.

DEN ALTEN

Then to old Uncle Emil
den du immer mimst
you always

missed,
missed most,
häng einem alten Haus

in fear, hung
from a rafter, a
beam old

Uncle Emil you
immer mimst
over the logical river

Fluss in the
truly really
feuchten clay, fucked finished clay.

LATE LOVE

Stuck in her stone hut
he fights to get the window up.

Her loopy Dachshunds
have made off with the pupils

of his eyes, like, or else
now from summit to summit

of whatever mountains against which
he thinks he hears the stars crash,

sounds truly *nada*
in all the sad façade.

AGAIN

The woman who
came out of the shadow

of the trees asked
after a time "what time is it"

her face
for a second

in my head
was there again

and I felt again
as against this emptiness

where also
I'd been.

WAITING

Waiting for the object,
the abject adjunct—

the loss of feel here,
field, faded.

Singing inside,
outside grey, wet,

cold out. The weather
doesn't know it,

goes only on to
wherever.

HANDS

Reaching out to shake,
take, the hand,

hands, take in
hand hands.

Three

"… come, poppy, when will you bloom?"
—Charles Olson

FATHERS

Scattered, aslant
faded faces a column
a rise of the packed
peculiar place to a
modest height makes
a view of common lots
in winter then, a ground
of battered snow crusted
at the edges under
it all, there under
my fathers their
faded women, friends,
the family all echoed,
names trees more tangible
physical place more tangible
the air of this place the road
going past to Watertown
or down to my mother's
grave, my father's grave, not
now this resonance of
each other one was his, his
survival only, his curious
reticence, his dead state,
his emptiness, his acerbic
edge cuts the hands to
hold him, hold on, wants
the ground, *wants* this frozen ground.

MEMORY GARDENS

Had gone up to
down or across dis-
placed eagerly
unwitting hoped for

mother's place in time
for supper just
to say anything
to her again one

simple clarity her
unstuck glued
deadness emptied
into vagueness hair

remembered wisp that
smile like half
her eyes brown eyes
her thinning arms

could lift her
in my arms so
hold to her so
take her in my arms.

FLICKER

In this life the
half moment
ago is just

at this edge
of curious place you
reach for feel

that instant shining
even still wet's
gone faded flashlight.

MY OWN STUFF

"My own stuff" a
flotsam I could
neither touch quite
nor get hold of, fluff,
as with feathers, milk-
weed, the evasive
lightness distracted yet
insistent to touch
it kept poking, trying
with my stiffened
fingers to get hold of
its substance I had
even made to be
there its only
reality my own.

WINDOW

The upper part is snow,
white, lower, grey
to brown, a thicket,
lacing, light seeming
hedge of branches, twigs,
growths of a tree, trees,
see eyes, holes, through
the interlacings, the white
emphatic spaced places
of the snow, the gravity,
weight, holds it, on top,
as down under, the grey,
brown, edged red, or
ground it has to come to,
must all come down.

WINTER MORNING

The sky's like a pewter
of curiously dulled blue,
and "My heart's in the highlands…,"
feels the day beginning again.

And whatever, whatever, says it
again, and stays here, stays
here with its old hands,
holds on with its stiff, old fingers,

can come too, like they say,
can come with me into this patient weather,
and won't be left alone, no, never alone ever again,
in whatever time's left for us here.

QUESTIONS

In the photograph you felt
grey, disregarded, your head
obscured by the company
around you, presuming
some awkward question. Were you dead?

Could this self-indulgence extend
to all these others, even
persuade them to do something
about you, or *with* you, given
they had their own things to do?

LOVERS

Remember? as kids
we'd looked in crypt
had we fucked? we
walked a Saturday
in cemetery it
was free the flowers
the lanes we looked
in past the small
barred window into
dark of tomb when
it looked out at us
face we saw white
looking out at us
inside the small
room was it man
who worked there? dead
person's fraught skull?

FUNERAL

Why was grandma
stacked in sitting room
so's people could come
in, tramp through.

What did we eat
that day before
we all drove off
to the cemetery in Natick

to bury her with grandpa
back where the small air-
port plane flew over
their modest lot there

where us kids could
look through the bushes,
see plane flying around or
sitting on the ground.

SUPPER

Time's more than
twilight mother at
the kitchen table over
meal the boiled potatoes
Theresa's cooked with meat.

CLASSICAL

One sits vague in this sullenness.
Faint, greying winter, hill
with its agéd, incremental institution,
all a seeming dullness of enclosure

above the flat lake—oh youth,
oh cardboard cheerios of time,
oh helpless, hopeless faith of empty trust,
apostrophes of leaden aptitude, my simple children,

why not anger, an argument, a proposal,
why the use simply of all you are or might be
by whatever comes along, your persons
fixed, hung, splayed carcasses, on abstract rack?

One instant everything must always change,
your life or death, your articulate fingers lost
in meat time, head overloaded, fused circuit,
all cheap tears, regrets, permissions forever utterly forgot.

MOTHER'S PHOTOGRAPH

Could you see present
sad investment of
person, its clothes,
gloves and hat,

as against yourself
backed to huge pine tree,
lunch box in hand in
homemade dress aged

ten, to go to school
and learn to be somebody,
find the way will
get you out of the

small place of home
and bring them with
you, out of it too,
sit them down in a new house.

VALENTINE

Had you a dress
would cover you all
in beautiful echoes
of all the flowers I know,

could you come back again,
bones and all,
just to talk
in whatever sound,

like letters spelling words,
this one says, *Mother,*
I love you—
that one, *my son.*

LECTURE

What was to talk to,
around in half-circle,
the tiers, ledges
of their persons

attending expectation,
something's to happen,
waiting for words,
explanations—

thought of cigarette
smoke, a puff recollected,
father's odor
in bed years ago.

BACK

Suppose it all turns into, again,
just the common, the expected
people, and places, the distance
only some change and possibly one

or two among them all, gone—
that word again—or simply more
alone than either had been
when you'd first met them. But you

also are not the same,
as if whatever you were were
the memory only, your hair, say,
a style otherwise, eyes now

with glasses, clothes even
a few years can make look
out of place, or where you
live now, the phone, all of it

changed. Do you simply give
them your address? Who?
What's the face in the mirror then.
Who are you calling.

KNOCK KNOCK

Say nothing
to it.
Push it away.
Don't answer.

Be grey,
oblique presence.
Be nothing
there.

If it speaks
to you, it
only wants
you for itself

and it has
more than you,
much
more.

HEAVY

Friend's story of dead whale on California beach
which the people blow up to get rid of and for weeks
after they're wiping the putrescent meat off their feet,

like, and if that's a heavy one, consider Meese
and what it takes to get rid of mice
and lice and just the nice people next door, *oh yeah*...

SKIN AND BONES

It ain't no sin
to sit down
take off your coat
wait for whatever

happens here
whenever it happens
for whatever.
It's your own skin.

THE DOCTOR

Face of my
father looks out

from magazine's
page on back

of horse at eight
already four

more than
I was when

the doctor died
as both

mother and Theresa
used to say, "the

doctor," whose
saddened son I

was and have
to be, my sister

older speaks of
him, "He felt

that with Bob
he was starting

over, perhaps, and
resolved not

to lose this son
as he had Tom and Phil…"

Nothing said
to me, no words more

than echoes, a
smell I remember

of cigarette box, a
highball glass,

man in bed with
mother, the voice

lost now. "Your
father was such

a Christmas fellow!"
So happy, empty

in the leftover
remnants of whatever

it was, the doctor's
house, the doctor's family.

LOST

One could reach up into
the air, to see if it was

still there, shoved back
through the hole, the little

purpose, hidden it was,
the small, persisting agencies,

arms and legs, the ears
of wonder covered with area,

all eyes, the echoes, the aches
and pains of patience, the

inimitable here and now of all,
ever again to be one and only one,

to look back to see the long distance
or to go forward, having only lost.

OLD

Its fears are
particular, head,

hands, feet, the
toes in two

patient rows,
and what comes

now is less,
least of all it

knows, wants in
any way to know.

THERE

On such a day
did it happen

by happy coincidence
just here.

LANGUAGE

Are all your
preoccupations un-

civil, insistent
caviling, mis-

taken dis-
criminating?

DAYS

for H.H.C.

In that strange light,
garish like wet blood,

I had no expectations
or hopes, nothing any more

one shouts at life to wake it up,
be nice to us—simply scared

you'd be hurt, were already
changed. I was, your head

out, looked— I want each
day for you, each single day

for you, give them
as I can to you.

HEAVENLY HANNAH

Oh Hannie
help me
help

Four

A Calendar

THE DOOR

Hard to begin
always again and again,

open that door
on yet another year

faces two ways
but goes only one.

Promises, promises...
What stays true to us

or to the other
here waits for us.

(*January*)

HEARTS

No end to it if
"heart to heart"
is all there is

to buffer, put against
harshness of this weather,
small month's meagerness —

"Hearts are trumps,"
win out again
against all odds,

beat this
drab season of bitter cold
to save a world.

(*February*)

MARCH MOON

Already night and day move
more closely, shyly, under this frozen

white cover, still rigid with
locked, fixed, deadened containment.

The dog lies snuffling, snarling
at the sounds beyond the door.

She hears the night, the new moon,
the white, wan stars, the

emptiness momently will break
itself open, howling, intemperate.

(March)

"WHAN THAT APRILLE..."

When April with his showers sweet
the drought of March has pierced to the root
and bathed every vein in such liqueur
its virtue thus becomes the flower...

When faded harshness moves to be
gone with such bleakness days had been,
sunk under snows had covered them,
week after week no sun to see,

then restlessness resolves in rain
after rain comes now to wash all clean
and soften buds begin to spring
from battered branches, patient earth.

Then into all comes life again,
which times before had one thought dead,
and all is outside, nothing in—
and so it once more does begin.

(April)

WYATT'S MAY

> In May my welth and eke my liff, I say,
> have stonde so oft in such perplexitie…
> —Sir Thos. Wyatt

In England May's mercy
is generous. The mustard

covers fields in broad swaths,
the hedges are white flowered—

but it is meager, so said.
Having tea here, by the river,

huge castle, cathedral, time
passes by in undigested,

fond lumps. Wyatt died
while visiting friends nearby,

and is buried in Sherborne Abbey
"England's first sonnet-maker…"

May May reward him and all
he stood for more happily now

because he sang May,
maybe for all of us:

"Arise, I say, do May some obseruance!
Let me in bed lie dreming in mischaunce..."

So does May's mind remember all
it thought of once.

(May)

SUMMER NIGHTS

Up over the edge of
the hill climbs the
bloody moon and

now it lifts the far
river to its old familiar
tune and the hazy

dreamlike field—and all
is summer quiet, summer
nights' light airy shadow.

(June)

"BY THE RUDE BRIDGE..."

Crazy wheel of days
in the heat, the revolution
spaced to summer's

insistence. That sweat,
the dust, time earlier they
must have walked, run,

all the way from Lexington
to Concord: "By the rude
bridge that arched the flood..."

By that enfolding small river
wanders along by grasses'
marge, by thoughtless stones.

(July)

VACATION'S END

Opened door chinks
let sun's restlessness

inside eighth month
going down now

earlier as day begins
later, time running down,

air shifts to edge
of summer's end

and here they've gone,
beach emptying

to birds, clouds,
flash of fish, tidal

waters waiting, shifting,
ripple in slight wind.

(August)

HELEN'S HOUSE

Early morning far trees lift
through mist in faint outline

under sun's first rose,
dawn's opalescence here,

fall's fading rush to color,
chill under the soft air.

Foreground's the planted small fruit trees,
cut lawn, the firs, as now

on tall dying tree beyond
bird suddenly sits on sticklike branch.

Walk off into this weather?
Meld finally in such air?

See goldenrod, marigold, yarrow, tansey
wait for their turn.

(September)

OLD DAYS

River's old look
from summers ago
we'd come to swim

now yellow, yellow
rustling, flickering
leaves in sun

middle of October
water's up, high sky's blue,
bank's mud's moved,

edge is
closer,
nearer than then.

(October)

THE TALLY

Sitting at table
wedged back against wall,

the food goes down in
lumps swallowed

in hunger, in
peculiar friendship

meets rightly again
without reason

more than common bond, the children
or the old cannot reach

for more
for themselves.

We'll wonder,
wander, in November,

count days and ways
to remember, keep away

from the tally,
the accounting.

(November)

MEMORY

I'd wanted
ease of year,
light in the darkness,
end of fears.

For the babe newborn
was my belief,
in the manger,
in that simple barn.

So since childhood
animals
brought back kindness,
made possible care.

But this world now
with its want, its pain,
its tyrannic confusions
and hopelessness,

sees no star
far shining,
no wonder as light
in the night.

Only us then
remember, discover,
still can care for
the human.

(December)

Windows

One

The Company

SONG

What's in the body you've forgotten
and that you've left alone
and that you don't want—

or what's in the body that you want
and would die for—
and think it's all of it—

if life's a form to be forgotten
once you've gone and no regrets,
no one left in what you were—

That empty place is all there is,
and/if the face's remembered,
or dog barks, cat's to be fed.

I WOULD HAVE KNOWN
YOU ANYWHERE

Back of the head, hand, the hair
no longer there, blown, the impotence
of face, the place no longer there, known
you were going to be there—

You were a character of dream,
a mirror looking out, a way
of seeing into space, an
impotent emptiness I share—

This day we spoke as number,
week, or time, this place an
absent ground, a house remembered
then no place. It's gone, it's gone.

What is it sees through, becomes
reflection, empty signal of the past,
a piece I kept in mind because
I thought it had come true?

I would have known you anywhere,
brother, known we were going to meet
wherever, in the street, this echo
too. I would have known you.

THE TERRIBLY STRANGE BED

I recall there being
portraits on the wall
with stiff, painted eyes
rolled round in the dark

on the wall across
from my bed and the other
in the room upstairs
where we all slept

as those eyes kept looking
the persons behind
about to kill me
only in sleep safe.

STAIRWAY TO HEAVEN

Point of hill
we'd come to, small
rise there, the friends
now separate, cars
back of us by
lane, the stones,

Bowditch, etc., location,
Tulip Path, hard
to find on the
shaft, that insistent
rise to heaven
goes down and down,
with names like floors,
ledges of these echoes,
Charlotte, Sarah,
Thomas, Annie
and all, as with
wave of hand I'd
wanted them one
way or other to
come, go with them.

INTERIOR

The room next to
this one with the lowered
lights, the kids watching
television, dogs squatted
on floor, and couch's
disarray, and all that
comes of living anywhere
before the next house, town,
people get to know you if
you let them, nowhere safe.

COMMON

Common's profound bottom
of flotsam, specious increase
of the space, a ground abounds,
a place to make it.

NOT MUCH

Not much you ever
said you were thinking
of, not much to
say in answer.

EPIC

Wanting to tell
a story,
like hell's simple invention, or
some neat recovery

of the state of grace,
I can recall lace curtains,
people I think I remember,
Mrs. Curley's face.

THE WORLD

The world so sweet its
saccharine outshot by
simple cold so colors
all against the so-called
starkness of the winter's
white and grey the
clouds the ice the
weather stables all in
flat particular light
each sunlit place so placed.

AFTER PASTERNAK

Think that it's all one?
Snow's thud, the car's
stuck door, the brilliant,
patient sun—

How many millions of years
has it been coming
to be here just this once—
never returning—

Oh dull edge of prospect—
weary window on the past—
whatever is here now
cannot last.

TREE

for Warren

You tree
of company—

here
shadowed branches,

small,
twisted comfortably

your size,
reddish buds' clusters—

all of
you I love

here
by the simple river.

BROAD BAY

Water's a shimmer,
banks green verge,
trees' standing shadowed,
sun's light slants,
gulls settle white
on far river's length.
All is in a windy echo,
time again
        a far sense.

JUST IN TIME
for Anne

Over the unwritten
and under the written
and under and over
and in back and in front of
or up or down or in
or in place of, of not,
of this and this, of
all that is, of it.

NATIONALGALERIE BERLIN

Nationalgalerie's
minute spasm's
self-reflective—
art's meager agony?

Two hundred years
zap past
in moment's
echoing blast!

No one apparently left
to say "hello"—
but for the genial
late Romanticists.

God, what a life!
All you see is *pain*.
I can't go through *that* again
—gotta go!

      •

Trying to get *image of man*
like trying on suit,
too small, too loose,
too late, too soon—

Wrong fit. Wrong time.

And you look out of
your tired head,
still stark naked,
and you go to bed.

      •

"Bellevue-Tower"
could be Brooklyn,
The roller skaters
go round and around on the plaza,

like "In Brueghel's great picture, The Kermess…"
Their rhythmic beauty
is so human, so human.
I watch and watch.

    .

Kids now with skateboards.
Edge of their chatter,
boys. voices changing,
lower, grow harsher.

This is the life of man,
the plans, the ways
you have to do it.
"Practice makes perfect."

    .

BY THE CANAL / SITTING

The rippled, shelved
surface of water,
quiet canal, the chunky
horse chestnut trees spread over
reflected in edge of darker
surface where else the light
shows in endless small rows
of slight, securing peace and quiet.

Further off, on each side,
cars, buses, trucks, bikes, and people.

But man and boy
pass back of me, spin of wheels,
murmur of their voices.

LIFE

for Basil

Specific, intensive clarity,
like nothing else
is anything
but itself—

so echoes all,
seen, felt, heard
or tasted, the one
and many. But

my slammed fist
on door, asking
meager, repentant entry
wants more.

DIALING FOR DOLLARS

CHOO CHOO

My mother just on edge
of unexpected death the
fact of one operation over
successful says, *it's all
free, Bob! You don't
have to pay for any of it!*
Life, like. Waiting for the train.

•

LIKE MINE

I'll always love
you no matter you
get all that money
and don't need a
helping hand like mine.

·

WAITING

I've never had the
habit of money but
have at times wanted
it, enough to give
myself and friends an
easy time over the
hump but you can
probably keep it, I'm
just here breathing, brother,
not exactly beside you.

·

THE WILLYS

Little
dollar
bills.

PICTURE

The scale's wrong. Kid's
leaned up against
Dad's huge leg, a

tree trunk, unfeeling bark,
rushing waters
of piss? Must be it

smells like toast,
like granular egg
or all night coffee

on all alone. All
so small,
so far to go.

LEAVING

Where to go
if into blank wall
and back of you
you can't get to—

So night is black
and day light,
ground, water
elemental.

It all accumulates
a place, something real
in place.
There it is—

till it's time to go,
like they say,
but the others
want to stay, and will.

NATURE MORTE

It's still
life. It
just ain't moving.

FLEURS

Clumped Clares.
Asphobellies.
Blumenschein.

THE COMPANY
for the Signet Society, April 11, 1985

Backward—as if retentive.
"The child is father to the man"
or some such echo of device,
a parallel of use and circumstance.

Scale become implication.
Place, postcard determinant—
only because someone sent it.
Relations—best if convenient.

"Out of all this emptiness
something must come…" Concomitant
with the insistent banality, small, still
face in mirror looks simply vacant.

Hence blather, disjunct, incessant
indecision, moving along on
road to next town where what waited
was great expectations again, empty plate.

So there they were, expectably ambivalent,
given the Second World War
"to one who has been long in city pent,"
trying to make sense of it.

We—*morituri*—blasted from classic
humanistic *noblesse oblige,* all the garbage
of either so-called side, hung on
to what we thought we had, an existential

raison d'être like a pea
some faded princess tries to sleep on,
and when that was expectably soon gone,
we left. We walked away.

Recorders ages hence will look for us
not only in books, one hopes, nor only under rocks
but in some common places of feeling,
small enough—but isn't the human

just that echoing, resonant edge
of what it knows it knows,
takes heart in remembering
only the good times, yet

can't forget whatever it was,
comes here again, fearing this
is the last day, this is the last,
the last, the last.

Two

Window

SCALES

for Buddy

Such small dimension
finally, the comfortable
end of it, the people
fading, world shrunk

to some recollected
edge of where it used to be,
and all around a sound
of coming, going. rustle

of neighboring movement out there
where as ever what one finally
sees, hears, wants, waits
still to recognize—is it

the sun? Grass, ground,
dog's bark. bird, the
opening, high clouds, fresh,
lifting day—*someone?*

XMAS

I'm sure there's a world I
can get to by walking another
block in the direction that
was pointed out to me by any-

one I was with and would even
talk to me that late at
night and with everything
confused—I know—the

kids tired, nerves stretched—
and all, and this person, old
man, Santa Claus! by
god—the reindeer, the presents.

WINDOW

THEN

The window had
been half
opened and the

door also
opened, and the
world then

invited, waited,
and one
entered

.

X

The world is
many, the

mind is
one.

.

WHERE

The window
opened,

beyond edge
of white hall,

light faint
shifts from back

a picture?
slurlike "wing"?

Who's
home?

            •

The roof's
above, old

reddish dulled
tiles, small

dormered windows, two
chimneys, above

the greyish,
close sky.

            ▪

Who's there,
old
question, who's
here.

.

Light's on
now

in three
sided balcony

window mid-
building, a floor

up from street.
Wait.

Watch it.
What light

on drab earth,
place on earth—

Continue?
Where to go so

far away
from here?

Friends?
Forgotten?

Movement?
A hand just

flesh, fingers?
White—

Who threads fantastic tapestry
just for me, for me?

.

WAITING

One could sit
minutes, hours,

days, weeks,
months, years—

all of its
rehearsal one

after one, be done
at last with it?

.

Or could go
in

to it, be
inside

head, look
at day

.

turn to dark,
get rid

of it at last, think
out

of patience, give
it up?

•

Man
with paper, white,

in hand
"tells the truth'

silent, moves
past the window

away—
sits down?

Comes back,
leans

forward at waist,

somewhat stiffly—
not

old,
young, young.

•

He must love someone
and this must be the story

of how he wanted
everything rightly done

but without the provision
planned, fell forward

into it all,
could not withstand

the adamant simplicity
of life's "lifelike" reality—

even in a mirror
replaced by another—

and couldn't wait
any longer,

must have
moved here.

To "live a life" alone?
to "come home"?

To be "lost and found"
again, "never more to roam"

again. Or something more like
"the fading light," like

they say, never quite
come. Never just one.

PLACE

Your face
in mind, *slow* love,

slow growing, *slow*
to learn enough.

Patience to learn
to be *here,* to savor

whatever there is
out there, without you

here, here
by myself.

NEW WORLD

Edenic land, Adamic person—
Foolishness is the price you'll have to pay
for such useless wisdom.

HO HO

for Joel

I have broken
the small bounds
of this existence and
am travelling south

on route 90. It
is approximately
midnight, surrogate
earth time, and you

who could, can, and
will never take anything
seriously will die
as dumb as ever

while I alone in
state celestial shoot
forward at designed rate,
speed at last unimpeded.

Three

Seven

SEVEN: A SUITE FOR ROBERT THERRIEN

STRAIGHT

They were going up in
a straight line right
to God, once they died—

The hills of home here
are a yellow pointer, again
God's simplistic finger—

Over the hill, the steeple
still glows in the late light—
all else whited out.

.

PLATE

All I ever wanted was
a place

up there
by myself.

.

"and the sky above—an old

blue

place" an

old

blue plate an old

blue face

.

Very carefully I
cut out an absolute

circle of blue
sky

or water. They
couldn't tell

the difference.

.

Blue plate

special

.

RED

When it goes
that fast

you don't see anything
but speed, you see

red.

.

I got something stuck
in my hand.

It was a splinter.

.

In the first World War
they had bombs

that looked like this.

.

How fast
do you think it's going?

.

SNOWMAN

Help the holes
be bigger. Put

your hand
in.

.

He grew a
point on

top
of his head—

two
of them.

·

That ice
cream cone'll

drip?

·

Curious
key hole.

·

I want to go into the immense
blue yonder

and I've built a negative number
times three.

·

WINGS

Those are hills out there
or mounds

Or breasts filling
the horizon.

·

It's a bird! Such
grace.

·

Sitting here
in Maine

I put you on the window sill
against the blue, white

yellow sky. You're a
sea gull suddenly.

What else
do I want.

·

Miles away they
are waiting for the promised

land again and the wind
has moved

the sand
into these shapes.

·

BOX

What do you think
he's got it for

unless
he means to use it.

·

No way
that could fit

(me)

.

"The worms
crawl in. The"

.

People walked
through the town carrying

coffins!

.

a *coffin*
fit...

Heh,
heh.

.

just stand him up
in the corner.

.

BOAT

Rock me, boat.
Open, open.

Hold me,
little cupped hand.

Let me come in,
come on

board you, sail
off, *sail off…*

H'S

Have Hannah's happy health —
have whatever, be

here, hombre… Her
hands upon edge

of table, her eyes
as dark centers, her

two teeth   but all,
her climbing, sacklike,

limp, her hands out-
stretched, or simply out

to it, her coming here,
her, all of her, her

words of her, *Hannah,
Hannie.* Good girl,

good. So we go
on with it. So is

Hannah
in this world.

AFTER FROST
for Sherman Paul

He comes here
by whatever way he can,
not too late,
not too soon.

He sits, waiting.
He doesn't know
why he should
have such a patience.

He sits at a table
on a chair.
He is comfortable
sitting there.

No one else
in this room,
no others, no expectations,
no sounds.

Had he walked
another way,
would he be here,
like they say.

BLACK GRACKLE
for Stan and Jane

Black grackle's refreshing eyeblink
at kitchen sink's
wedged window—
a long way to go after all,

a long way back to the crack
in some specific wall
let the light in, so
to speak— Let the bird *speak,*

squeak prettily, and sit
on my finger, pecking ring's blue
stone. Home, home all around here,
geese peer in, goats graze, I suppose

they eat, want no
arbitrary company nor summary
investigation pretends in any way
so to know them—and give milk.

Youth has its own rewards,
and miles to go before I sleep
is echo of miles and miles,
wherever, whatever it was—

I wanted you and *you*
sat down to stay awhile.
If all there was was such
one pulled the threads and all

fell out, if going there was only
coming here with times between
and *everyday a holiday with Mary*
and *I love you still* and *always will,*

then *then* could not begin again
its busyness, its casual consequences,
and no head on no shoulders, *no*
eyes or ears, etc., nothing forward

in this peculiarly precious instance
scrunched down here, screaming—ultimate *me*—
for miles and miles around
its devastating sound.

THE SEASONS

for Jasper Johns

"Therefore all seasons will be sweet to thee..."
—S. T. Coleridge, "Frost at Midnight"

Was it *thunk* suck
of sound an insistent

outside into the patience
abstract waited was lost

in such simple flesh *où*
sont les mother and

father so tall the green
hills echoéd and light

was longer, longer, into
the sun, all the small

body bent at last to
double back into one

and one and one wonder,
paramour pleasure.

•

High air's lightness heat
haze grasshopper's chirr

sun's up hum two close
wet sweat time's hung in space

dust deep greens a wave of grasses
smells grow faint sounds echo

the hill again up and down
we go—

*summer, summer, and not even
the full of it…*

Echoes again body's time a
ticking a faint insistent

intimate skin wants weather
to reassure.

•

All grown large world
round *ripeness is all*

an orange pumpkin harsh
edge now of frost an

autumnal moon over the
far off field leads back

to the house all's dead
silence the peculiarly

constructed one you were
all by yourself   *Shine on*

Hear the walls of fall
The dark flutes of autumn

sound softly… Oh love,
love, remember me.

·

As if because or
whenever it was it was

there again muffled mute
an extraordinary quiet

white and cold far off
hung in the air without

apparent edge or end
nowhere one was or if

then gone waited
come full circle again

deep and thick and even
again and again

having thought to go nowhere
had got there.

·

The seasons, tallies of earth,
keep count of time,
say what it's worth.

SIGHT

Eye's reach out window water's
lateral quiet bulk of trees at
far edge now if peace were
possible here it would enter.

.

Bulk of trees' tops mass of
substantial trunks supporting from
shifting green base lawn variable
greens and almost yellow looks like.

.

Seven grey metal canoes drawn
up and tethered by pond's long
side with brushy green bushes and
metallic light sheen of water at evening.

.

What see what look for what
seems to be there front of the fore-
head the echoing painful minded
ness of life will not see this here.

Four

Dreams

DREAMS

What you think you
eat at some table like
a pig with people
you don't even

know and lady there
feeds you all and you,
finally you at least
are full, say, look at

them still eating! Why
(says a woman, another
sitting next to me) those
others still eating you

so cannily observed are
unlike you who *could* be fed
because you were hungry! But
them, they can't—they

are possessed by the
idea of hunger, *never* enough
to eat for them, agh…
Or you either, dreamer,

who tells this simple
story being all these
same offensive persons
in one empty head.

•

In dreams begin the
particulars of those
echoes and edges,

the quaint ledges of
specific childhood nailed
to my knees and

leaning in unison
while the other
men went off, the

women working, the
kids at baleful
play, mud-colored

with rocks and stones and
trees years ago in
Albuquerque, New Mexico we'd

stopped the night I dreamt
I was to be child forever
on way to get the kids from camp.

                    .

Have you ever
had vision as if

you were walking
forward to some

edge of water through
the trees, some country

sunlit lane, some
place was just ahead

and opening as your body
elsewise came

and you had
been in two places?

FOR THE WORLD THAT EXISTS

No safer place to live than with children
for the world that exists.

IF

Up the edge of the window out to
tree's overhanging branches sky
light on facing building up to
faint wash blue up on feet ache
now old toes wornout joints make
the wings of an angel so I'd fly.

LIGHTS

I could get
all of it.

I could say
anything.

I wish I could
just get even.

I'm here.
I'm still here.

When did
it happen.

Where was
everyone.

I wish I could
just get even.

Now you've
gone away.

Nobody
wants to stay.

Here I am.
Here I am.

I DREAMT

I dreamt I dwelt in a big building—
four walls, floor and a ceiling,
bars in front and behind.
Nothing on my mind

I dreamt I dwelt in a can,
round, tin, sides, top and bottom,
and I couldn't get out.
Nobody to get me out.

I dreamt I dwelt in marble halls,
a men's room with a trough
you pissed in, and there I was.
There were a lot of us.

I dreamt I dwelt in a house,
a home, a heap of living
people, dogs, cats, flowers.
It went on for hours.

Whatever you dream is true.
It's just you making it up,
having nothing better to do.
Even if you wanted to, you couldn't.

SPARKS STREET ECHO

Flakes falling
out window make
no place, no place—

no faces, traces,
wastes of whatever
wanted to be—

was here
momently, mother,
was here.

YOU

You were leaving, going
out the door in

preoccupation as to
what purpose it

had served, what
the point was, even

who or what or where,
when you thought you

could, suddenly, say
you understood, and

saw all people as if
at some distance, a

pathetic, vast huddle
up against a fence.

You were by no means
the Cosmic Farmer

nor Great Eyeball in Sky.
You were tired, old now,

confused as to purpose,
even finally alone.

You walked slowly
away or rather got in

the car was waiting
with the others.

How to say clearly what
we think so matters

is bullshit, how all the
seeming difference is none?

Would they listen, presuming
such a *they*? Is any-

one ever home to such in-
sistences? How ring

the communal bell?
All was seen in

a common mirror, all
was simple self

reflection. It was me
and I was you.

FOCUS

Patches of grey
sky tree's

lines window
frames the

plant hangs
in middle.

PLAGUE

When the world has become a pestilence,
a sullen, inexplicable contagion,

when men, women, children
die in no sense realized, in

no time for anything, a
painful rush inward, isolate—

as when in my childhood the
lonely leper pariahs so seemingly

distant were just down the street,
back of drawn shades, closed doors—

no one talked to them, no one
held them anymore, no one waited

for the next thing to happen—as
we think now the day begins

again, as we look for the faint sun,
as they are still there, we hope, and we are coming.

AGE

Most explicit—
the sense of trap

as a narrowing
cone one's got

stuck into and
any movement

forward simply
wedges one more—

but where
or quite when,

even with whom,
since now there is no one

quite with you— Quite? Quiet?
English expression: *Quait?*

Language of singular
impedance? A dance? An

involuntary gesture to
others *not* there? What's

wrong here? How
reach out to the

other side all
others live on as

now you see the
two doctors, behind

you, in mind's eye,
probe into your anus,

or ass, or bottom,
behind you, the roto-

rooter-like device
sees all up, concludes

"like a worn out inner tube,"
"old," prose prolapsed, person's

problems won't do, must
cut into, cut out...

The world is a round but
diminishing ball, a spherical

ice cube, a dusty
joke, a fading,

faint echo of its
former self but remembers,

sometimes, its past, sees
friends, places, reflections,

talks to itself in a fond,
judgmental murmur,

alone at last.
I stood so close

to you I could have
reached out and

touched you just
as you turned

over and began to
snore not unattractively,

no, never less than
attractively, my love,

my love—but in this
curiously glowing dark, this

finite emptiness, *you, you, you*
are crucial, hear the

whimpering back of
the talk, the approaching

fears when I may
cease to be me, all

lost or rather lumped
here in a retrograded,

dislocating, imploding
self, a uselessness

talks, even if finally to no one,
talks and talks.

FUNNY

Why isn't it funny when you die,
at least lapse back into archaic pattern,
not the peculiar holding on to container
all other worlds were thought to be in—

archaic, curious ghost story then,
all sitting in the familiar circle,
the light fading out at the edges,
and voices one thinks are calling.

You watch them go first, one by one,
you hold on to the small, familiar places,
you love intently, wistfully, now
all that you've been given.

But you can't be done with it
and you're by no means alone.
You're waiting, watching them go,
know there's an end to it.

Five

Eight Plus

IMPROVISATIONS
for Lise Hoshour

YOU BET

Birds like
windows.

·

YONDER

Heaven's up
there still.

·

THE KIDS

Little
muffins

in a
pan.

·

THE CART

Oh well, it
thinks.

·

NEGATIVE

There's a big
hole.

•

SITE

Slats in
sunlight a
shadow.

•

PURITAN

Plant's in
place.

•

VIRTUES

Tree limbs'
patience.

•

CARS

Flat out
parking lot.

•

BLUE

Grey blue
sky blue.

•

HOLES

Sun's
shining through

you.

•

TEXAS REVERSE

You all
go.

•

ECHOES

"All god's
children got—"

•

OLD SONG

"Some sunny
day—"

•

YEAH

Amazing grace
on Willy's face!

·

HELP

This here
hand's out.

·

SEE

Brown's another
color.

·

DOWN

It's all
over
the floor.

·

WINDOW

Up from reflective
table top's glass the
other side of it.

·

AROUND

The pinwheel's pink
plastic spinning
blade's reversing.

.

EGO

I can
hear l can
see

.

DAYTIME

It's got to be
lighter.

.

SPACE

Two candles
light brown—
or yellow?

.

WINDOW SEAT

Cat's up
on chair's edge.

.

EYES

All this
color's yours.

.

GREEN

Plant's tendrils
hanging from

but not
to—

.

SEASCAPE

Little boat
blue blown
by bay.

.

BIT

"De
sign ~~Qu~~
art
e[a]rly"

.

GROUP

"AL
 APHIC
 Y"

•

WEIGH

Rippled refractive
surface leaves
light lights.

•

THE EDGE

"Your
 Mem
 Is Enc

•

QUOTE

"a lot
 of thought-
 ful people"

•

GHOST

What you don't
see you
hear?

　　　•

TEACHER

The big
red
apple.

　　　•

CANDLE HOLDER

Small glass
cube's opaque
clarity in
window's light.

　　　•

FIELDS

Meadows
more at home.

　　　•

TABLE TOP

Persian's
under glass.

WHEELS

for Futura 2000

One around one—
or inside, limit
and dispersal.

Outside, the emptiness
of no edge, round
as the sky—

Or the eye seeing
all go by
in a blur of silence.

OH

Oh stay awhile.
sad, sagging flesh
and bones gone brittle.

Stay in place,
aged face, teeth,
don't go.

Inside and out
the flaccid change
of bodily parts,

mechanics of action,
mind's collapsing
habits, all

echo here
in mottled skin, blurred eye,
reiterated mumble.

Lift to the vacant air
some sigh, some sign
I'm still inside.

READING OF EMMANUEL LEVINAS

> "He does not limit knowledge
> nor become the object of thinking..."
> —Krzystztof Ziarek

Thought out of self
left beyond the door

left out at night
shuttered openness

dreams dream of dreaming
inside seeming outside

since left then gone
comes home alone.

     •

Puts hands down
no river one place

step over into
the ground sense

place was will be
here and now

nowhere can be
nothing's left.

.

Outside forms distance
some hundred feet

away in boxed air across
bricked enclosed space

a horizontal young woman
blue coat red pants

asleep on couch seen
through squared window

five floors up in form
above's blue sky

a lateral cloud
air of solemn thinking.

.

Who else was
when had they come

what was the program
who was one

why me there
what other if

the place was determined
the deed was done?

WATER

Your personal world echoes
in ways common enough,
a parking lot, common cold,
the others sitting at the table.

I have no thoughts myself,
more than myself. I feel
here enough now to think
at least I am here.

So you should get to
know me? Would I be
where you looked? Is it
hands across this body of water?

Is anyone out there,
they used to say, or was
they also some remote chance
of people, a company, together.

What one never knows is,
is it really real, is
the obvious obvious, or else
a place one lives in regardless.

CONSOLATIO

What's gone is gone.
What's lost is lost.

What's felt as pulse—
what's mind, what's home.

Who's here, where's there—
what's patience now.

What thought of all,
why echo it.

Now to begin—
Why fear the end.

WHAT

What would it be
like walking off
by oneself down

that path in the
classic woods the light
lift of breeze softness

of this early evening and
you want some time
to yourself to think

of it all again
and again an
empty ending?

SENATOR BLANK BLANK

I look at your
bland, piglike
face and hear

your thin-lipped,
rhetorical bullshit
and wonder if anyone

can or will believe you,
and know they do,
just that I'm listening to you too.

BETTER

Would it be better
piecemeal, a little
now and then, or

could one get inside
and hide there, wait
for it to end.

No one's doing anything to you.
It's just there's nothing
they can do for you.

Better with dignity to die?
Better rhetoric would clarify.
"Better Business Bureaus" lie.

WALL

You can push as hard as you want
on this outside side.

It stays limited
to a single face.

USA

Seeing with Sidney people
asleep on floor of subway—

myself worrying about time—
how long it would take to get to the plane—

How far in the universe to get home,
what do you do when you're still alone,

what do you say when no one asks,
what do you want you don't take—

When train finally comes in,
there's nothing you're leaving, nothing you can.

FOR AN OLD FRIEND

What became of your novel with the lunatic
mistaken for an undercover agent,

of your investment of the insistently vulnerable
with a tender of response,

your thoughtful wish that British letters
might do better than Peter Russell—

Last time I saw you, protesting
in London railway station

that all was changed,
you asked for a tenner

to get back to Bexhill-on-Sea.
Do you ever think of me.

HERE

In other
words opaque
disposition intended
for no one's interest
or determination
forgotten ever
increased but
inflexible and
left afterwards.

EARS IDLE EARS
for Susan

Out one
ear and
in the
other ear
and out
without it.

BLUE MOON

The chair's still there,
but the goddamn sun's
gone red again—

and instead of Mabel
there is a potato,
or something like that there,

sitting like it owned the place.
It's got no face
and it won't speak to anyone.

I'm scared.
If I had legs,
I'd run.

ECHO

Rudimentary characteristic of being
where it has to be, this tree

was where it was
a long time before anything else

I know or thought to.
Now it's pushed out by people—

rather by their effects, the weakening
the insistent wastes produce.

Where can anyone go
finally if the damn trees die

from what's done to them—what
being so called *alive* has come to?

What's left after such death.
If nothing's there, who's here.

FAMOUS LAST WORDS
for John Chamberlain

PLACE

There's a way out
of here but it

hurts at the edges
where there's no time left

to be one if
you were and friends

gone, days seemingly
over. No one.

·

LATE

Looks like chunks
will be it

tonight, a bite-sized
lunch of love,

and lots of it,
honey.

·

VERDE

Green, how I love you green…
the prettiest color I've ever seen,

the way to the roses through them stems,
the way to go when the light changes!

What grass gets when you water it,
or the folding stuff can get you in,

but finally it's what isn't dead
unless it's skin with nothing under it—

or faces green from envy or hunger or fear,
or some parallel biological fact, my dear.

·

BOZO

Bill's brother was partial
to windows, stood on boxes

looking over their edges.
His head was

higher than his shoulders,
but his eyes were

somewhere down under
where he thought he could

see it all now, all
he'd wanted to, aged four,

looking up under skirts,
wearing ochre-trim western shirts.

Regular slim-jim ranchero,
this vicious, ambitious, duplicitous, no

wish too late, too
small, bozo.

．

MILES

Simple trips, going
places, wasted
feelings, alone
at last, all the rest

of it, counting, keeping
it together, the weather,
the particular people, all
the ways you have to.

．

NIGHT LIGHT

Look at the light
between the lights

at night with the lights
on in the room you're sitting

in alone again with
thc light on trying still

to sleep but bored and
tired of waiting up late

at night thinking of some
stupid simple sunlight.

.

ECHOES (1)

Patience, a peculiar
virtue, waits in time,

depends on time to
make it, thinks it

can have everything
it wants, wants all

of it and echoes dis-
appointment, thinks

of what it thought
it wanted, nothing else.

.

ECHOES (2)

This intensive going in,
to live there, in

the head, to wait
for what it seems

to want, to look
at all the ways

of looking, seeing
things, to always

think of it, think
thinking's going to work.

.

LIFE

All the ways to go,
the echoes, made sense.

It was as fast as that,
no time to figure it out.

No simple straight line,
you'd get there in time

enough standing still.
It came to you

whatever you planned to do.
Later, you'd get it together.

Now it was here.
Time to move.

.

FAMOUS LAST WORDS

Which way did they go?
Which way did they come.

If it's not fun, don't do it.
But I'm sure you wouldn't.

You can sum it all up in a few words
or less if you want to save time.

No wisdom hasn't been worn out
by simple repetition.

You'll be with me till the end?
Good luck, friend.

ECHOES

for William Bronk

The stars stay up there where they first were.
We have changed but they seem as ever.

What was their company first to be, their curious proposal,
that we might get there which, of course, we did.

How dead now the proposal of life simply, how echoing it is,
how everything we did, we did and thought we did!

Was it always you as one, and them as one,
and one another was us, we thought, a protestant, a complex

determination of this loneliness of human spaces.
What could stars be but something else no longer there,

some echoing light too late to be for us specific.
But there they were and there we saw them.

EIGHT PLUS

Inscriptions for Eight Bollards
at 7th & Figueroa, LA
                  for James Surls

What's still here settles
at the edges of this
simple place still
waiting to be seen.

                ·

I didn't go
anywhere and
I haven't
come back!

                ·

You went by so
quickly thinking
there's a whole world
in between.

                ·

It's not a
final distance,
this here
and now.

                ·

How much I would
give just to know
you're standing in
whatever way here.

.

Human eyes
are lights to me
sealed
in this stone.

.

No way to
tell you anything
more than
this one.

.

You walk tired
or refreshed, are
past in a moment,
but saw me.

.

Wish happiness
most for us,
whoever we are,
wherever.

.

If I sit here
long enough,
all will pass me by
one way or another.

·

Nothing left out,
it's all in a heap,
all the people
completed.

·

Night's eye is
memory
in day-
light.

·

I've come and gone from here
with no effect,
and now feel
no use left.

·

How far from
where it
was I'll
never know.

·

You there
next to the others
in front of
the one behind!

.

No one speaks
alone. It
comes out
of something.

.

Could I think
of all you
must have felt?
Tell me.

.

What's inside,
what's the place
apart from
this one?

.

They say this
used to be
a forest
with a lake.

.

I'm just
a common
rock,
talking.

.

World's
still got
four
corners.

.

What's
that
up there
looking down?

.

You've got a nice
face and
kind eyes and
all the trimmings.

.

We talk like
this too
often someone
will get wise!

Six

Helsinki Window

"Even if he were to throw out by now absolutely incomprehensible stuff about the burning building and look upon his work simply as an effort of a carpenter to realize a blueprint in his mind, every morning he wakes up and goes to look at his house, it is as if during the night invisible workmen had been monkeying with it, a stringer has been made away with in the night and mysteriously replaced by one of inferior quality, while the floor, so meticulously set by a spirit level the night before, now looks as if it had not even been adjudged by setting a dish of water on it, and cants like the deck of a steamer in a gale. It is for reasons analogous to this perhaps that short poems were invented, like perfectly measured frames thrown up in an instant of inspiration and, left to suggest the rest, in part manage to outwit the process."

—Malcolm Lowry,
*Dark As the Grave
Wherein My Friend Is Laid*

X

The trees are kept
in the center of the court,
where they take up room
just to prove it—

and the garbage cans extend
on the asphalt at the far side
under the grey sky and the building's
recessed, regular windows.

All these go up and down
with significant pattern,
and people look out of them.
One can see their faces.

I know I am safe here
and that no one will get me,
no matter where it is
or who can find me.

HELP

Places one's come to
in a curious stumble, things
one's been put to, with,
in a common bundle

called suffering humanity
with faces, hands
where they ought to be,
leaving usual bloody traces.

I like myself, he thought, but
it was years and years ago
he could stand there watching
himself like a tv show.

Now you're inside entirely,
he whispers in mock self-reassurance,
because he recognizes at last, by god,
he's not all there is.

SMALL TIME

Why so curiously happy
with such patient small agony
not hurting enough
to be real to oneself—

or even intimidated
that it's at last too late
to make some move
toward something else.

Late sun, late sun,
this far north you still shine,
and it's all fine,
and there's still time enough.

BIENVENU

for the company
of Lise Hoshour, Philippe Briet,
Michel Butor, and Robert Therrien:
"7&6," Philippe Briet Gallery,
NYC, October 7, 1988

Welcome to this bienfait
ministry of interior muses,
thoughtful provocateurs, etc.

All that meets your eye
you'll hear with ear
of silent surprises

and see these vast surmises
bien entendu by each
autre autrefois. Our

welcome so to you
has come— Mon frère, mon semblable,
and sisters all.

     •

Thoughtful little holes in
places makes us
be here.

Empty weather makes
a place of faces
staring in.

Come look at
what we three
have done here.

"EVER SINCE HITLER..."

Ever since Hitler
or well before that
fact of human appetite
addressed with brutal
indifference others
killed or tortured or ate
the same bodies they
themselves had we ourselves
had plunged into density
of selves all seeming stinking
one no possible way
out of it smiled or cried
or tore at it and died
apparently dead at last
just no other way out.

THINKING

I've thought of myself
as objective, viz.,
a thing round which
lines could be drawn—

or else placed by years, the average
some sixty, say, a relative
number of months, days,
hours and minutes.

I remember thinking of war
and peace and life
for as long as I can remember.
I think we were right.

But it changes, it thinks
it can all go on forever
but it gets older.
What it wants is rest.

I've thought of place
as how long it takes
to get there and of where
it then is.

I've thought of clouds, of water
in long horizontal bodies, or
of love and women and the children
which came after.

Amazing what mind makes
out of its little pictures,
the squiggles and dots,
not to mention the words.

CLOUDS

The clouds passing over, the
wisps still seeming substantial, as
a kid, as a kid I'd see them up there

in the town I grew up in on the hills
in the fields on the way home then
as now still up there, still up there.

ALL WALL

Vertical skull time
weather blast bombastic disaster impasse time,
like an inside out and back down again design,
despair ready wear impacted beware scare time—

like old Halloween time,
people all gone away and won't be back time,
no answer weeks later empty gone out dead
a minute ahead of your call just keeps on ringing time—

I'm can't find my way back again time,
I'm sure it was here but now I can't find it time,
I'm a drag and sick and losing again wasted time,
You're the one can haul me out and start it over again

Time. Too much time too little
not enough too much still to go time,
and time after time and not done yet time
nothing left time to go time. Time.

WHATEVER

Whatever's
to be
thought
of thinking
thinking's
thought of
it still
thinks
it thinks
to know
itself so
thought.

188

Thought so
itself know to
thinks it
thinks still it
of thought
thinking's
thinking
of thought
be to
whatever's.

KLAUS REICHERT AND
CREELEY SEND REGARDS
in memory LZ

Nowhere up there enough
apart as surmised see my
ears feel better in the
air an after word from Romeo's
delight spells *the* and *a*
aged ten forever friend
you'll know all this by heart.

ECHOES

What kind of crows,
grey and black, fussy
like jays, flop
on the tree branches?

"What kind of
love is this" flops
flat nightly, sleeps
away the days?

What kind of place
is this? What's out there
in these wet unfamiliar
streets and flattened,

stretched faces?
Who's been left here,
what's been wasted
again.

FOOLS

1

Stripped trees in the wet wind,
leaves orange yellow, some still green,
winter's edge in the air,
the close, grey sky...

Why not be more
human, as they say,
more thoughtful,
why not try to care.

The bleak alternative's
a stubborn existence—
back turned to all,
pathetic resistance.

2

You'd think the fact
another's tried it
in the common world
might be a language

like the animals
seem to know
where they've come from
and where they'll go.

Curse the fool
who closes his sad door—
or any other more
still tries to open it.

MEAT

Blood's on the edge of it
the man with the knife cuts into it

the way out is via the door to it
the moves you have mean nothing to it

but you can't get away from it
there's nothing else left but it

have you had enough of it
you won't get away from it

this room is thick with it
this air smells of it

your hands are full of it
your mouth is full of it

why did you want so much of it
when will you quit it

all this racket is still it
all that sky is it

that little spot is it
what you still can think of is it

anything you remember is it
all you ever got done is always it

your last words will be it
your last wish will be it

The last echo it last faint color it
the drip the trace the stain—it.

NEW YEAR'S RESOLUTION

What one might say
wanting to do it,
hoping to solve it,
make resolution—

You break it to bits,
swallow the pieces,
finally quit quitting,
accept it, forget it.

But what world is this
has such parts,
or makes even thinkable
paradoxic new starts—

Turn of the year
weighs in the cold
all that's proposed
simply to change it.

Still, try again
to be common, human,
learn from all
how to be one included.

THE DRUNKS OF HELSINKI

Blue sky, a lurching tram makes
headway through the small city.
The quiet company sits shyly,
avoiding its image, else talks

with securing friends. This
passage is through life as if
in dream. We know our routes
and mean to get there. Now

the foetid stink of human excess,
plaintive, and the person beside us
lurches, yet stays stolidly there.
What are the signals? Despair,

loss of determinants—or a world
just out of a bottle? Day
after day they clutter the tram
stops, fall sodden over seats

and take their drunken ease in
the fragile world. I think, they
are the poets, the maledictive,
muttering words, fingers pointing,

pointing, jabbed outright across
aisle to blank side of bank or
the company's skittish presence.
I saw a man keep slamming the post

with his fist, solid in impact,
measured blows. His semblable sat
slumped in front of me, a single seat.
They meet across the aisle in ranting voices,

each talking alone. In a place of
so few words sparely chosen, their
panegyric slabbering whine has human
if unexpected resonance. They

speak for us, their careful friends, the sober
who scuttle from side to side in vacantly
complex isolation, in a company has compact
consensus, minds empty of all conclusion.

HELSINKI WINDOW
for Anselm Hollo

Go out into brightened
space out there the fainter
yellowish place it
makes for eye to enter out
to greyed penumbra all the
way to thoughtful searching
sight of all beyond that
solid red both brick and seeming
metal roof or higher black
beyond the genial slope I
look at daily house top on
my own way up to heaven.

.

Same roof, light's gone
down back of it, behind
the crying end of day, "I
need something to do," it's
been again those other
things, what's out there,
sodden edge of sea's
bay, city's graveyard, park
deserted, flattened aspect,
leaves gone colored fall
to sidewalk, street, the end
of all these days but
still this regal light.

.

Trees stripped, rather shed
of leaves, the black solid trunks up
to fibrous mesh of smaller
branches, it is weather's window,
weather's particular echo, here
as if this place had been once,
now vacant, a door that had had
hinges swung in air's peculiar
emptiness, greyed, slumped elsewhere,
asphalt blank of sidewalks, line of
linearly absolute black metal fence.

.

Old sky freshened with cloud bulk
slides over frame of window the
shadings of softened greys a light
of air up out of this dense high
structured enclosure of buildings
top or pushed up flat of bricked roof
frame I love *I love* the safety of
small world this door frame back
of me the panes of simple glass yet
airy up sweep of birch trees sit in
flat below all designation declaration
here as clouds move so simply away.

•

Windows now lit close out the
upper dark the night's a face
three eyes far fainter than
the day all faced with light
inside the room makes eye re-
flective see the common world
as one again no outside coming
in no more than walls and post-
card pictures place faces across
that cautious dark the tree no
longer seen more than black edge
close branches somehow still between.

•

He was at the edge of this
reflective echo the words blown
back in air a bubble of suddenly
apparent person who walked to
sit down by the familiar brook and
thought about his fading life
all "fading life" in tremulous airy
perspect saw it hover in the surface
of that moving darkness at the edge
of sun's passing water's sudden depth
his own hands' knotted surface the
sounding in himself of some other.

·

One forty five afternoon red
car parked left hand side
of street no distinguishing
feature still wet day a bicycle
across the way a green door-
way with arched upper window
a backyard edge of back wall
to enclosed alley low down small
windows and two other cars green
and blue parked too and miles
and more miles still to go

·

This early still sunless morning when a chair's
creak translates to cat's cry a blackness still
out the window might be apparent night when the
house still sleeping behind me seems a bag of
immense empty silence and I feel the children
still breathing still shifting their dreams an
enigma will soon arrive here and the loved one
centers all in her heavy sleeping arm out the
leg pushed down bedclothes this body unseen un-
known placed out there in night I can feel all
about me still sitting in this small spare pool of
light watching the letters the words try to speak.

.

Classic emptiness it
sits out there edge of
hierarchic roof top it
marks with acid fine edge
of apparent difference it
is *there* here *here* that
sky so up and out and where
it wants to be no birds no
other thing can for a
moment distract it be
beyond its simple space.

WHAT

What had one thought the
outside was but place all
evident surface and each
supposed perspect touched
texture all the wet implicit
world was adamant edge of
limit responsive if indifferent
and changing (one thought) in-
side its own evident kind one
banged upon abstract insens-
itive else echoed in passing
was it the movement one's own?

VOICE

Bears down on
the incisive way to
make a point common
enough speaking
in various terms it
says the way of
satisfaction is a
lowly thing echo
even wants to can
come along alone in-
clusion also a way
particularizing life.

SO MUCH

When he was a kid sick
in bed out the window
the clouds were thick and
like castles, battlements he'd
think he could climb up to
them, a veritable jack in
the beanstalk high there with
sun and blue air he'd never
need anything more again to
get well, so it had to fade
away, whatever that old voice
enlarges, so much to depend upon.

ECHO

for J. L.

Outside the
trees
make limit of
simple

sight. The
weather is
a grey, cold on
the

skin. It feels
itself
as if a place it
couldn't

ever get to
had been at
last
entered.

WINTER NIGHT

Building's high bulk lifts
up the mass is lighter in this
curiously illumined darkness air
somehow fragile with the light is
beyond again in yellow lit win-
dows frame of the bars and behind
a seeming room the lamp on the
table there such peculiar small
caring such signs five floors up
or out window see balcony's iron
frame against snowed roof's white
or pinkish close glow all beyond.

FADING LIGHT

Now one might catch it see it
shilt almost substantial blue
white yellow light near roof's edge
become intense definition think
of the spinning world is it as
ever this plate of apparent life
makes all sit patient hold on
chute the sled plunges down ends
down the hill beyond sight down
into field's darkness as time for
supper here left years behind waits
patient in mind remembers the time.

OLD MISTER MOONLIGHT

Split broken un-
circumvented excised
walked out door snow
day freaking thoughts
of empty memory back
past time gone undone
left car side pool
of greying edged
rings fledged things
wedged buildings all
patterns and plans fixed
focus death again.

FOR J.L.

The ducks are gone
back to the pond, the echo

of it all a curious
resonance now it's

over, life's like that?
What matters, so soon become fact.

NIGHT

This bluish light behind the block of
building this familiar returning
night comes closer this way can sit
looking see the bulk of it take shape
in front of the sky comes now up from
behind it up to mount its light its
yellow quiet squares fix a front in

the dark to be there make a static
place looks like home in dark's
ambivalence sit down to stay awhile
places there black's dominance a shade it
rides to closes it shuts it finally off.

MARCH

Almost at the dulled
window fact the wet
birches soften in melt-
ing weather up still from
far ground the backyard
asphalt grey plastic garbage
bins the small squat
blackened pile of stubborn
snow still sit there echo
of fading winter all the days
we waited for this side
of spring changes everything

FIRST LOVE

Oh your face is there a mirror days
weeks we lived those other places in
all that ridiculous waste the young we
wanted not to be walked endless streets
in novels read about life went home at
night to sleep in tentative houses left
one another somewhere now unclear no per-
sons really left but for paper a child or
two or three and whatever physical events
were carved then on that tree like initials
a heart a face of quiet blood and somehow
you kept saying and saying an unending pain.

SPRING LIGHT

Could persons be as this
fluffed light golden spaces
intent airy distances so up
and out again they are here
the evening lowers against the sun
the night waits far off at the
edge and back of dark is summer's
light that slanting clarity all
wonders come again the bodies open
stone stillness stunned in the silence
hovering waiting touch of air's edge
piece of what had not been lost.

Echoes

… Sea, hill and wood,
This populous village! Sea, and hill, and wood,
With all the numberless goings on of life,
Inaudible as dreams! the thin-blue flame
Lies on my low-burnt fire, and quivers not;
Only that film, which fluttered on the grate,
Still flutters there, the sole unquiet thing.
Methinks, its motion in this hush of nature
Gives it dim sympathies with me who live,
Making it a companionable form,
Whose puny flaps and freaks the idling Spirit
By its own moods interprets, every where
Echo or mirror seeking of itself,
And makes a toy of Thought.

—S. T. Coleridge,
"Frost at Midnight"

One

MY NEW MEXICO
for Gus Blaisdell

Edge of door's window
sun against
flat side adobe,
yellowed brown—

A blue lifting morning,
miles of spaced echo,
time here plunged
backward, backward—

I see shadowed leaf
on window frame green,
close plant's growth,
weathered fence slats—

All passage explicit,
the veins, hands,
lined faces crease,
determined—

Oh sun! Three years,
when I came first,
it had shone unblinking,
sky vast aching blue—

The sharpness of each
shift the pleasure,
pain, of particulars—
All inside gone out.

Sing me a song
makes beat specific,
takes the sharp air,
echoes this silence.

BRICK

Have I bricked up unbricked what
perspective hole break of eye
seen what glowing place what
flower so close grows from a
tiny brown seed or was it what
I wanted this after imaged green
round sun faints under blue sky
or outer space that place no
one knows but for this echo of
sketched in color the stems of
the voluptuous flowers patient
myself inside looking still out.

BOWL

He comes she comes carrying carrying
a flower an intense interest a color
curious placed in an outer an inner
ring of rounded spaces of color it
looked this way they say it was here
and there it was it opened opens color
it sees itself seen faithful to echo
more than all or was the green seeming
back of it fragile shoots a way it was
yellow banded together zigzagged across
as a box for it wants to touch touches
opens at the edges a flower in a bowl.

SHADOW

There is a shadow
to intention a place
it comes through and
is itself each stasis
of its mindedness ex-
plicit walled into
semblance it is a
seemingly living place
it wants it fades it
comes and goes it puts
a yellow flower in a pot
in a circle and looks.

FIGURE OF FUN

Blue dressed aged blonde
person with pin left
lapel hair bulged to
triangular contained wide
blue grey eyed now
authority prime minister
of aged realm this
hallowed hollowed ground
lapped round with salted water
under which a tunnel runs
to far off France and history
once comfortably avoided.

WALDOBORO EVE

Trees haze in the fog coming in,
late afternoon sun still catches the stones.

Dog's waiting to be fed by the empty sink,
I hear the people shift in their rooms.

That's all finally there is to think.
Now comes night with the moon and the stars.

OLD

Framed roof slope from tower's window
out to grey wet field with green growth,
edge again of midfield hedgerow and trees beyond,
the tugging familiar, the fading off fogged distance—

Are these memories already?
Does it seem to me I see what's there.
Have I particulars still to report,
is my body myself only?

Hear the cricket, the keening slight
sound of insect, the whirring of started
vacuum cleaner, television's faint voices now
down below. Here is world.

OLD WORDS

The peculiar *fuck it*
cunt shit violence
of a past learned in
school all words only
one by one first heard
never forgotten as recall
head or heart vagaries
a dusk now so early
in the afternoon the wet
feel of days socks touch
of things said to me
forever please *fuck me.*

TRANSLATION

You have all the time been
here if not seen, not thought
of as present, for when I
looked I saw nothing, when
I looked again, you had
returned. This echo, sweet
spring, makes a human sound
you have no need of, facts
so precede, but you hear, you
hear it, must feel the intent
wetness, mushy. I melt again
into your ample presence.

SELF PORTRAIT

This face was detachable
as blurred head itself
lifted from old bookcover
library yielded a faded
years ago image graced
now newspaper's rushed
impression static glossed
sentiment "life" a few hours
more to "live" till wrapped
tight round fresh loaf delivered
come home eaten comes to rest
on yesterday's garbage.

HERE AGAIN

He was walking
toward the other in-
viting him for-
ward now with an
eager antici-
pation he could rec-
ognize if not al-
together trust him-
self with any-
one else still
waiting also
to be met.

ECHO

Entire memory
hangs tree
in mind to see
a bird be—

but now puts stutter
to work, shutters
the windows, shudders,
sits and mutters—

because can't
go back, still
can't get
out. Still can't.

PURE

Why is it *pure*
so defeats, makes
simple possibility
cringe in opposition—

That bubbling, mingled
shit with water
lifted from bathtub's
drain hole's no

stranger to me,
nor ever in mind
blurred image, words
won't say what's

asked of them. I
think the world I think,
wipe my relentless ass,
wash hands under faucet.

EYES

I hadn't noticed that
building front had narrow
arrowlike division going
up it the stairwell at
top a crest like spearpoint
red roofed it glistens
with rain the top sharply
drawn horizontal roof edge lets
sky back there be a faint
blue a fainter white light
growing longer now higher
going off out of sight.

SOME

You have not simply
insisted on yourself
nor argued
the irrelevance

of any one else. You
have always wanted
to be friends, to be
one of many.

Persuaded
life even
in its largeness
might be brought

to care, you
tried to make it
care, humble, illiterate,
awkward gestured.

So you thought,
as inevitable age approached,
some loved you,
some.

You waited for
some wind
to lift, some
thing to happen,

proving it finally,
making sense more
than the literal,
still separate.

ECHO

White light blocked
impulse of repose like
Wouldn't you tell me
what you were doing   Couldn't
I go where you go   Faith
you kept secretly because it
had no other place to be   My

217

eyeball's simple hole wherein
'the gold gathered the
glow around it'   All you
said you wanted fainted
All the ways to say   No

THERE

Seeming act
of thought's
gagging

insight out
there's spasmodic
patience a wreck

car's hauled
now away
another day's

gone to hell
you know like
hangs out.

HERE ONLY

Why does it cry so much
facing its determined despair—
As woman locked in cage—
child—or eyes only left to look—
Why—   What wanted—   Why is it
this way or that way thrashes
stubborn only in its absence—

It was never there—was only
here to be itself—here only this
one chance to be—   Cannot live
except it finds a place given—
Open to itself only as any—

IT

Nothing there
in absence as,
unfelt, it
repeated itself—

I saw it,
felt it,
wanted
to belt it—

Oh love, you
watch, you
are so
"patient"—

Or what
word makes my
malice
more.

DEATH

Unlet things
static dying
die in common
pieces less
crescendo
be it simple
complex death
a physical
world again un-
ended unbegun to
any other world
be this one.

HERE AND NOW

Never other than this unless
is counted sudden, demanded
sense of falling or a loud,
inexplicable yell just back
of ears, or if the tangible
seeming world rears up dis-
torted, bites hands that would
feed it, can feel no agreeable
sensation in the subject's hard-
ly learned vocabulary of social
moves, agreements, mores—
then up shit creek sans paddle.

ABSTRACT

The inertia unexpected of
particular reference, it
wasn't where you said it
would be, where you looked
wasn't where it was! What
fact of common world is
presumed common? The
objectifying death of all
human person, the ground?
There you are and I look
to see you still, all
the distance still implacable.

THE CUP

Who had thought
echo precedent,

shadow the seen
thing, action

reflective—
whose thought was

consequential,
itself an act, a

walking round rim
to see what's within.

CHAIN

Had they told you, you
were "four or more cells
joined end to end," the Latin,
catena, "a chain," the loop,
the running leap to actual
heaven spills at my stunned
feet, pours out the imprison-
ing threads of genesis,
oh light beaded necklace,
chain round my neck, my
inexorably bound birth, the sweet
closed curve of fading life?

EAST STREET

Sense of the present
world out window, eye's
blurred testament

to "St Francis Xavier's
School," red brick
and grey cornices,

the snow, day old,
like thin, curdled milk,
God's will high

above on cross
at church top over
embedded small arches

and close, tiled
roof. The cars
parked, the accelerating

motor of one
goes by, the substantial
old birch, this

closer look—
path Dennis shoveled—
distraction of all report.

BAROQUE

Would you live your life spectrum
of fly sealed in amber block's
walk the patient fixed window see
days a measure of tired time a
last minute thought of whatever not
now remembered lift up sit down
then be reminded the dog is your
paradigm seven years to one all
reckoned think out muse on be sud-
denly outside the skin standing
upright pimpled distinction chilled
independence found finally only one?

FOR NOTHING ELSE

For nothing else,
this for love

for what other
one is this

for love once
was and is

for love,
for love.

PARTS

for Susan Rothenberg

HUMAN LEG GOAT LEG

Which the way echoed
previous cloven-hoofed
dark field faint formed
those *goat men leading her*
in physical earth's spring
jumps one-legged parallel
long walked thinned out
to sparse grounded skin
bones of what scale say
now goat transforms man
then man goat become
and dances dances?

SNAKE FISH BIRD

Archaic evolving thing
in all surface all beginning
not hair or any seeming simple
extension bring to mind pattern
of woven wetnesses waste a streak
of wonder of evil tokens the underneath
beside ground's depths spoken
low in sight soundless in height
look past reflection see the light
flash of finned ripple wing
this ancient *Fellow* follow
to weather, to water, to earth.

HORSE LEG DOG HEAD

Its mute uncute cutoff
inconsequent eye slot
centuries' habits accumulate
barks the determined dog
beside horse the leg the
walking length the patent
patient slight bent limb
long fetlock faith faint
included instructions placed
aside gone all to vacant
grass placed patiently thus
foot's function mind's trust.

DOG LEG WHEEL

Four to the round
repetitive inexorable
sound the wheel the whine
the wishes of dogs
that the world be real
that masters feel
that bones be found
somewhere in the black ground
in front or in back
before and behind
hub for a head bark's
a long way back. And on

GOAT'S EYE

Eye hole's peculiar framed
see you, want you, think
of eye out, lost last sight,
past goat thoughts, what
was it, when or why—
Or if still the stiff
hair, musk, the way
eye looks out, black
line contracted, head's skull
unstudied, steady,
it led to lust, follows
its own way down to dust.

DOG HEAD WITH RABBIT LEG

Break the elliptical
make the face deadpan tell
nothing to it smile for the
camera lie down and roll over
be in complex pieces for once
you ran the good race broke
down and what's left you
least of all can understand.
It was cold. It was hard.
Dogs barked. Rabbits ran.
It comes to such end,
friend. Such is being dead.

DOG HEAD WITH CRESCENT MOON

Harvested this head's
a manifest of place the
firmament's fundament.
Overhead sky's black night
in lieu of echoed moon
seems sounding out
a crescent crescendo
for a dog's life.
Barked bones soft
mouth's brought home
the arc again the light.
Waits patient for reward.

BIRD AND CALF

Peculiar patience is death
like an envelope a flap
a postulate you'd left a
space where it was and it
has gathered the outside
of its body in or just
flopped down dropped all
alternative forever waiting
for the plummeting streak
gets closer closer and
the god who cleans up things
puts death to work.

Had never known blue air's
faded fascination had never
seen or went anywhere never
was a horse unridden but on
one proverbial frosty morning
whilst going to the kitchen
I thought of our lives' opaque
addiction to distances to
all the endless riders etched
on those faint horizons and
nuzzled the mere idea of you—
swapped breath. *Oh love, be true!*

Two

WHITE FENCE / WHITE FENCE
(for Paul Strand's photograph "White Fence")

Particularizing "White
Fence" beyond which
the seeming

echoes of barn, house,
bright light flat
on foursquare

far building while
in closer view shades
darken the faint ground.

Yet *fence* as
image or word,
white or black, or

where place the person,
the absent,
in this ring of focus?

I come closer, see
in *there* the
wistful security,

all in apparent place,
the resonant design, diamond,
the *dark/light,*

the way all plays to pattern,
the longed for world
of common facts.

Then this *fence* again,
as if pasted on,
pushes out and across,

a static, determined
progress of detailing
edges, *American,* an

odd reason so forced
to be seen. It
cannot accommodate,

cannot let get past,
unaffected, any, *must* be
"White Fence."

EAST STREET AGAIN

for Carl Rakosi

The tree stands clear in the weather
by the telephone pole, its stiff brother.
Hard to think which is the better,
given living is what we're here for
and that one's soon dead no matter.
Neither people nor trees live forever.
But it's a dumb thought, lacking other.
Only this passing faint snow now for tether—
mind's deadness, emptiness for pleasure—
if such a flat, faint echo can be measure.
So much is forgotten no matter.
You do what you can do, no better.

SONNETS
for Keith and Rosmarie

Come round again the banal
belligerence almost a
flatulent echo of times
when still young the Sino
etc conflict starvation lists
of people without work or place
world so opaque and desperate
no one wanted even to
go outside to play even
with Harry Buddy who hit
me who I hit stood slugging
while they egged us on.

·

While ignorant armies clash
bash while on the motorway
traffic backed up while they
stand screaming at each other
while they have superior
armaments so wage just
war while it all provokes
excuses alternatives money
time wasted go tell it
on the town dump deadend
avoidance of all you might
have lived with once.

·

Someone told me to stand
up to whoever pushed me
down when talking walking
hand on friend's simple
pleasures thus abound when
one has fun with one
another said surrogate
God and planted lettuce
asparagus had horses cows
the farm down the road
the ground I grew up
on unwon unending.

.

I'd take all the learned
manner of rational un-
derstanding away leave
the table to stand on
its own legs the plates
to stick there the food
for who wants it the places
obvious and ample and
even in mind think it
could be other than an
argument a twisting
away tormented unless.

.

Me is finally unable having
as all seem to ended with
lost chances happily enough
missed the boat took them
all to hell on a whim
went over whatever precipice
but no luck just stupid
preoccupation common
fear of being overly hurt
by the brutal exigencies were
what pushed and pulled
me too to common cause.

                    .

So being old and wise and
unwanted left over from
teeth wearing hands wearing
feet wearing head wearing
clothes I put on take now
off and sleep or not or sit
this afternoon morning night
time's patterns look up at
stars overhead there what
do they mean but how useless
all violence how far away you
are from what you want.

                    .

Some people you just
know and recognize,
whether a need or fact,
a disposition at that
moment is placed,
you're home, a light
is in that simple
window forever—   As if
people had otherwise always
to be introduced, told
you're ok—   But here
you're home, so longed
for, so curiously
without question found.

OTHER

Having begun in thought there
in that factual embodied wonder
what was lost in the emptied lovers
patience and mind I first felt there
wondered again and again what for
myself so meager and finally singular
despite all issued therefrom whether
sister or mother or brother and father
come to love's emptied place too late
to feel it again see again first there
all the peculiar wet tenderness the care
of her for whom to be other was first fate.

BODY

Slope of it,
hope of it—
echoes faded,
what waited

up late inside
old desires
saw through
the screwed importunities.

This regret?
Nothing's left.
Skin's old,
story's told—

but still touch,
selfed body,
wants other,
another mother

to him, her
insistent "sin"
he lets in
to hold him.

Selfish bastard,
headless catastrophe.
Sans tits, cunt,
wholly blunt—

tucked it up,
roof top, loving cup,
sweatered room,
old love's tune.

Age dies old,
both men and women cold,
hold at last no one,
die alone.

Body lasts forever,
pointless conduit,
floods in its fever,
so issues others parturient.

Through legs wide,
from common hole site,
aching information's dumb tide
rides to the far side.

"YOU WERE NEVER LOVELIER..."
for Cletus

Inside that insistence—
small recompense— Persistence—
No sense in witless
thoughtlessness, no one

has aptitude for waiting—
hating, staying away later,
alone, left over, saw
them all going

without her (him), wanted
one for him (her)self, left
on the shelf, "them" become
fact of final indifference—

The theme is thoughtlessness,
the mind's openness, the
head's large holes, the gaps
in apparent thinking. So that

amorphic trucks drive through
you, mere, mired, if unmoved,
agency, left by the proposed "they"
to stay, alone of all that was.

The world is, or seems, entirely
an aggression, a running over, an
impossible conjunct of misfits
crash about, hurting one another.

No names please, no no one or someone.
Say goodbye to the nonexistent—never
having lived again or ever, mindless—
trucks, holes, clouds, call them—

those sounds of shapes in tides of space—
pillaging weather, shifting about one
or two or simply several again, an issue
only of surmise, a surprise of

sunset or sunrise, a day or two can't
think about or move out, or be again certain,
be about one's own business, be vanity's own simpleton,
simply, *You Were Never Lovelier*...

REFLECTION

It must be low key
breeze blowing through
room's emptiness is
something to think of—

but not enough
punch, pain enough,
despair to make
all else fade out—

This morning, that
morning? Another ample
day in the diminishing
possibility, the

reflective reality
alters to place
in specific place
what can't get past.

THE OLD DAYS

Implicit echo of the
seemingly friendly
face and grace as well
to be still said. Go to hell

(or heaven), old American
saying—   My sister's friends
are affectionate people,
and also seemingly real.

Can I calculate—as to say,
can I still stay up late
enough to catch Santa Claus or
New Year's, are the small, still

tenets of truth still observable—
And how is your mother? Dead, sir,
these less than twenty years.
The voice echoes the way it was—

And if I am mistaken, sir.
If I am thought in error, was the error
intentional, did I mean to confuse you.
Were the great waves of myriad voices too

much of enough—   You remember Cocteau's *A little
too much is enough for me*—   Tits were beautiful—
bubbles of unstable flesh, pure, tilting pleasure.
You cannot finally abjure beauty

nor can you simply live without it—
reflective, beating your meat, unspeakable,
light headed with loneliness. Oh to be old
enough, fall down the stairs, break everything—

One often did but in such company
was heaven—   Breath, arms, eyes,
and consummate softness—   Breathing softness,
moist, simply conjoining softness, like a pillow.

No man is an island, no woman a pillow—
Nobody's anything anymore. Was it Pound
who said, *The way out is via the door*—
Do they say that anymore—

Do I hear what I hear. Then where
are the snows of yesteryear,
the face that sank a thousand ships,
all that comforting, nostalgic stuff

we used to hear. Sitting in company
with others, I look at the backs
of my hands, see slightly mottled,
swollen flesh, hear difficultly

through many voices—see a blur.
Yet you were, you are here—
If I am a fool in love,
you'll never leave me now.

YOUR

One sided
battering ramm'd
negligible asset
carnal friend—

Patience's provision
test of time
nothing ventured
nothing gained—

In the fat doldrums
of innocent aging
I sat waiting—
Thank god you came.

GNOMIC VERSES

LOOP

Down the road Up the hill Into the house
Over the wall Under the bed After the fact
By the way Out of the woods Behind the times
In front of the door Between the lines Along the path

ECHO

In the way it was in the street
it was in the back it was
in the house it was in the room
it was in the dark it was

FAT FATE

Be at That this
Come as If when
Stay or Soon then
Ever happen It will

LOOK

Particular pleasures weather measures or
Dimestore delights faced with such sights.

HERE

Outstretched innocence
Implacable distance
Lend me a hand
See if it reaches

TIME

Of right Of wrong Of up Of down
Of who Of how Of when Of one
Of then Of if Of in Of out
Of feel Of friend Of it Of now

MORAL

Now the inevitable
As in tales of woe
The inexorable toll
It takes, it takes.

EAT

Head on backwards
Face front neck's
Pivot bunched flesh
Drops jowled brunch.

TOFFEE

Little bit patted pulled
Stretched set let cool.

CASE

Whenas To for
If where From in
Past place Stated want
Gain granted Planned or

HAVE A HEART

Have heart Find head
Feel pattern Be wed
Smell water See sand
Oh boy Ain't life grand

OH OH

Now and then
Here and there
Everywhere
On and on

WINTER

Season's upon us
Weather alarms us
Snow riot peace
Leaves struck fist.

DUTY

Let little Linda allow litigation
Foster faith's fantasy famously
And answer all apt allegations
Handmake Harold's homework handsomely

GOTCHA

Passion's particulars
Steamy hands
Unwashed warmth
One night stands

WEST ACTON SUMMER

Cat's rats, Mother's brother
Vacation's patience, loud clouds
Fields far, seize trees
School's rules, friends tend
Lawn's form, barn's beams
Hay's daze, swallows follow
Sun's sunk, moon mends
Echo's ending, begin again

FAR

"Far be it from Harry to alter the sense of drama
inherent in the almighty tuxedo…"

"Far be it from Harry"
Sit next to Mary
See how the Other
Follows your Mother

PAT'S

Pat's place
Pattern's face
Aberrant fact
Changes that

FOUR'S

Four's forms
Back and forth
Feel way Hindside
Paper route Final chute

SENTENCES

Indefatigably alert when hit still hurt.
Whenever he significantly alters he falters.
Wondrous weather murmured mother.
Unforgettable twist in all such synthesis.
Impeccably particular you always were.
Laboriously enfeebled he still loved people.

WORDS

Driving to the expected
Place in mind in
Place of mind in
Driving to the expected

HERE

You have to reach
Out more it's
Farther away from
You it's here

DATA

Exoneration's face
Echoed distaste
Privileged repetition
Makeshift's decision—

.

Now and then
Behind time's
Emptied scene and
Memory's mistakes—

．

You are here
And there too
Being but one
Of you—

SCATTER

All that's left of coherence.

ECHO AGAIN

Statement keep talking
Train round bend over river into distance

DOOR

Everything's before you
were here.

SUMMER '38

Nubble's Light a sort
of bump I thought—
a round insistent
small place

not like this—
it was a bluff,
tip on the edge
of the sea.

AIR

Lift up so you're
Floating out
Of your skin at
The edge but
Mostly up seeming
Free of the ground.

ECHOES

Think of the
Dance you could do
One legged man
Two legged woman.

THERE

Hard to be unaddressed—
Empty to reflection—
Take the road east—
Be where it is.

ECHOES

Sunrise always first
That light—is it
Round the earth—what
Simple mindedness.

STAR

Where
It is
There
You are

·

Out there
In here
Now it is
Was also

·

Up where
It will be
And down
Again

·

No one
Point
To it
Ever

ECHO

Brutish recall
seems useless now
to us all.

But my teeth you said
were yellow
have stayed nonetheless.

It was your handsomeness
went sour, your
girlish insouciance,

one said.
Was being afraid
neurotic?

Did you talk of it.
Was the high cliff jumpable.
Enough enough?

Fifty years
have passed.
I look back,

while you stand here,
see you there, still
see you there.

THINKING OF WALLACE STEVENS

After so many years the familiar
seems even more strange, the hands

one was born with even more remote, the feet
worn to discordant abilities, face fainter.

I love, loved you, Esmeralda, darling Bill.
I liked the ambience of others, the clotted crowds.

Inside it was empty, at best a fountain in winter,
a sense of wasted, drab park, a battered nonentity.

Can I say the whole was my desire?
May I again reiterate my single purpose?

No one can know me better than myself,
whose almost ancient proximity grew soon tedious.

The joy was always to know it was the joy,
to make all acquiesce to one's preeminent premise.

The candle flickers in the quick, shifting wind.
It reads the weather wisely in the opened window.

So it is the dullness of mind one cannot live without,
this place returned to, this place that was never left.

A NOTE

I interrupt these poems to bring you some lately particular
information, which is that such coherence or determining
purpose as I presumed myself to have in a collection such as
this (not very long ago at all) seems now absent. Thus I col-
lect much as a magpie (in Duncan's engaging sense) all that
attracts me. Be it said once again that writing is a pleasure.
So I am not finally building roads or even thinking to per-
suade the reader of some conviction I myself hold dear. I
am trying to practice an art, which has its own insistent au-
thority and needs no other, however much it may, in fact,
say. I had not really understood what the lone boy
whistling in the graveyard was fact of. Now I listen more
intently.

ALEX'S ART

Art's a peculiar division of labors—"a small town cat before he
        [joined the band"—
as if the whole seen world were then an echo

Of anyone's mind in a past tense of Arabs, say,
inventing tents in the early hours of meager history.

It is "an ever fixed mark," a parallel, "blue
suede persuasion," a thing out there beyond

Simple industries and all those sad captains thereof.
It is a place elsewhere, time enough, "please

Pass the bacon" again, oh finite, physical person.
Listen to the wonders of how it's been, or how it is

And will be, now as sky lifts the faint edge of morning in yellowish
    [grey tones,
as I hear nothing, as I listen again, brought into myself,

As all of it now tails back of me in flooded pockets,
as even the hum of the machine, call it, sings its persistent song—

As each so-called moment, each plunge and painful recovery
of breath echoes its precedent, its own so-called raison d'être,

Arch or meager, living or forgotten, here or finally there,
its it thinks the givens, feels around for place to put them down,

No metaphoric by-pass, no hands in pockets, no home alone,
no choice, nowhere to sit down. But what is immensely evident,

Even in each particular such as always that "where are the snows of
    [yesteryear,"
is why pay so painfully in advance for what can never be here now?

Look at it this way. You know those simple coordinates of A and B.
Add C, the comedian. Add X and Y. Add the apparent sun and
    [simple sky.

Add everything and everyone you've ever known. Still empty? Still
only time enough to settle the bills, or try to, to be kind to the dog
    [who waits?

Trees' edges defined more now as sun lifts, lifted, to higher point
     [in far off space.
I see this world as a common picture, having among others two
          [dimensions

As well as a presently pleasant odor like, say, fresh cut hay. I hear
          [little,
given my ears are not working quite properly, and I have gone
          [indoors

A long, long way down a tunnel to where my TV sits on a table,
and I sit before it, watching the news. All a world in mind, isn't it,

As we do or do not get the bad guys? I don't know. But I still can
          [see,
and I look at you. The simple question still. Can you see me?

DUTCH BOY

I'd thought
boy caught stopped

dike's dripping water
with finger

put in hole
held it all back

oh hero
stayed steadfast

through night's black
sat waited

till dawn's light
when people came

repaired the leak
rescued

sad boy. But
now I see what

was the fact
he was stuck

not finger in hole was
but he could not

take it out
feared he'd be caught

be shamed
blamed

so sat
through the night

uncommonly distraught
in common fright.

FRAGMENT

Slight you lift.
Edge skin down.
Circle seen.
Places now found.

Featured face.
Hand in when.
Disposition.
Distrust.

Three

FAINT FACES

I can't move
as formerly but
still keep
at it as the

ground cants
rising to manage
some incumbent
cloud of

reference left
years back
the tracks absent
events it

was part of
parting and
leaving still
here still there.

TIME

How long for the small yellow flowers
ride up from the grasses' bed,
seem patient in that place—

What's seen of all I see
for all I think of it—
but cannot wait, no, *cannot* wait.

The afternoon, a time, floats
round my head, a boat I float on,
sit on, sat on, still rehearse.

I seem the faded register, the misplaced camera,
the stuck, forgotten box, the unread book,
the rained on paper or the cat went out for good.

Nowhere I find it now or even
stable within the givens, thus comfortable to reason,
this sitting on a case, this fact sans face.

THIS HOUSE

Such familiar space
out there, the window
frame's locating

focus I could
walk holding
on to

through air from
here to there,
see it where

now fog's close
denseness floats
the hedgerow up

off apparent ground,
the crouched, faint
trees lifting up

from it, and more
close down
there in front

by roofs slope, down,
the stonewall's conjoining,
lax boulders sit,

years' comfortable pace
unreturned, placed
by deliberation and

limit make their
sprawled edge. Here
again inside

the world one thought of,
placed in this aged box
moved here from

family site
lost as us, time's
spinning confusions

are what
one holds on to.
Hold on, dear house,

'gainst the long hours
of emptiness, against
the wind's tearing force.

You are my mind
made particular
my heart in its place.

THE ROAD

Whatever was else or less
or more or even
the sinister prospect
of nothing left,

not this was anticipated,
that there would be no one
even to speak of it.
Because all had passed over

to wherever they go.
Into the fiery furnace
to be burned to ash.
Into the ground,

into mouldering skin and bone
with mind the transient guest,
with the physical again dominant
in the dead flesh under the stones.

Was this the loved hand, the
mortal "hand still capable of grasping…"
Who could speak
to make death listen?

One grows older,
gets closer.
It's a long way home,
this last walking.

THE PLACE

Afternoon it changes
and lifts, the heavy
fog's gone and the wind

rides the field, the flowers,
to the far edge
beyond what's seen.

It's a dream
of something or
somewhere I'd been

or would be, a place
I had made
with you, marked out

with string
years ago. Hannah
and Will are

no longer those
children
simply defined.

Is it weather
like wind blows, and all
to the restless sea?

PERSONAL

"Urgent" what the message says.
First of all purposes.
The loss of place for porpoises.
Less use of detergents.

Lack luster linens.
Tables without chairs.
Passionate abilities given little leeway.
They never were.

Thirties a faded time.
Forties the chaos of combat.
Fifties lots of loneliness.
Sixties redemption.

I look at you.
You look at me.
We see.
We continue.

PARADE

Measure's inherent
in the weight,
the substance itself
the person.

How far, how
long, how high,
what's there
now and why.

Cries in the dark,
screams out,
silence,
throat's stuck.

Fist's a weak grip,
ears blotted with echoes,
mind fails focus
and's lost.

Feet first,
feet last,
what difference,
down or up.

You were the shape
I took in the dark.
You the me
apprehended.

Wonders!
Simple fools,
rulers, all of us
die too.

On the way
much happiness
of a day,
no looking back.

ONWARD

"We cannot give you any support
if we don't know who you are."

You cannot drive on this road
if you do not have a car.

I cannot sleep at night
if I won't go to bed.

They used to be my friends
but now they are dead.

ONE WAY

Oh I so
like the
avoidance
common

to patient
person stands
on curb waiting
to cross.

Why not run out
get clobbered truck
car or bus
busted

to bits
smiling even
in defeat
stay simple.

Such sizing up
of reality
whiff of reaction
you will not

walk far alone
already the crowd
is with you or else
right behind.

I see you
myself sit
down walk too
no different

just the patient
pace we keep
defeats us
in the street.

THE WORDSWORTHS
for Warren

The Wordsworths afoot
fresh fields' look.

birds hop on gravestone
small lake beyond

up long dank road
Coleridge's home—

Out this window I see
a man turning hay

early sun's edge
strike the green hedge

a blue round of field flower
mark the fresh hour

high spike of mullein
look over walled stone—

House slope blacked roof
catches eye's proof

returns me to day
passed far away

Dorothy took note,
William wrote.

HERE

Seen right of head,
window's darkening outlook
to far field's slope
past green hedgerow.

Here, slanted lengthening
sun on back wall's
dancing shadows,
now comes night.

FIVE VARIATIONS ON "ELATION"
for Bill McClung

This sudden
uplift elation's
pride's brought out!

Even ambiguity's
haughtily exalted oh
rushed, raised spirit.

        •

Rushed unexpected my
heart leaps up when
I behold the sudden
as in the common.

        •

Curiously with pride
above common lot to walk,

to be lifted up
and out, exalted:

        •

His elation was brief?
Brought back to earth,

still for a time
it was otherwise.

        •

Faded but unforgotten
if down once
uplifted if unsure
once proud if
inside once out.

.

ECHO

Elation's ghost
dance echoes
little, leaves no
traces, counts
no number—

Wants from no
one privilege. Has
no pride by being it.
If then recognized,
needs no company.

What wind's echo,
uplifted spirit?
Archaic feelings
flood the body.
Ah! accomplished.

EDGES

for Pen's birthday (everyday)

Edges of the field, the blue flowers, the reddish wash of
the grasses, the cut green path up to the garden
plot overgrown with seedlings and weeds—

green first of all, but light, the cut of the sunlight
edges each shift of the vivid particulars, grown large
—even the stones large in their givens, the shadows massing

their bulk, and so seeing I could follow out to another
edge of the farther field, where trees are thick on the sky's
edge, thinking I am not simply a response to this, this light,

not just an agency sees and vaguely adumbrates, adds an opinion.
There is no opinion for life, no word more or less general.
I had begun and returned, again and again, to find you finally,

felt it all gather, as here, to be a place again, and wanted to
shuck the husk of habits, to lift myself to you in this sunlight.
If it is age, then what does age matter? If it is older or younger,

what moment notes it? In this containment there cannot
be another place or time. It all lives by its being
here and now, this persistent pleasure, ache of promise, misery
    [of all that's lost.

Now as if this moment had somehow secured to itself a body,
had become you, just here and now, the wonders inseparable
in this sunlight, *here*, had come to me again.

BILLBOARDS

AGE

Walking on
the same
feet
birth

provided,
I is not
the simple
question

after all,
nor *you*
an interesting
answer.

MORAL

Practice
your humility
elsewhere
'cause it's just another

excuse for privilege,
another place not
another's, another
way you get to get.

BIG TIME

What you got
to kill now isn't
dead enough
already? Wait,

brother, it *dies,* it
no way can *live*
without you, it's
waiting in line.

ECHO

It was a thoughtful
sense of paced
consideration,
whatever the agenda

had prompted as
subject. "Here we
are," for example, or
"There they were"…

So all together now,
a deep breath, a
fond farewell.
Over.

TRUE OR FALSE

"One little
freckle
houses
bacteria

equal
to the population
of New York—"
You cannot

breath, scratch
or move
sans killing
what so

lives on you
There are
no vacancies, no
rooms with a view.

DREAM

What's the truth
for except it
makes a place for
common entrances, an

old way home down
the street 'midst faces,
the sounds' flooding
poignance, the approach?

SKY

Now that the weather softens the
end of winter in the tips of
trees' buds grow lighter a yellow
air of lifting slight but persistent
warmth you walk past the street's
far corner with turbanlike color swathed
hat and broad multicolored shawl hangs
down over your trunklike blue cloth
coat with legs black dog's tugging
pull on leash's long cord I walk quickly
to catch up to you pulled equally by
your securing amplitude, blue love!

A BOOK

for Pam and Lew

A book of such
sweetness the
world attends
one after

another a found
explicit fondness
mends the tear
threads intercross

here where there
repairs a cluster
comes mitigates
irritation reads words.

A VIEW AT EVENING

Cut neat path out
to darkening
garden plot
old field's forgot.

Far hedge row's
growth goes
down the hill
where blurred

trees depend,
find an end
in distance
under dark clouds.

The upright space,
place, fades sight,
sees echoes,
green, green, green.

THIS ROOM

Each thing given
place in the pattern
rather find
place in mind

a diverse face
absent past
shelf of habits
bits pieces

eye lost then
love's mistakes
aunt's battered house
off foundation

children's recollection
tokens
look back
chipped broken

room goes on
dark winter's edge
now full with sun
pales the worn rug.

SINS

A hand's part,
mouth's open look,
foot beside
the long leg.

Away again.
Inside the house
open windows
look out.

It was fun.
Then it's gone.
Come again
some time.

TIME'S FIXED

Time's fixed
as ticking instrument,
else day's insistent
ending into

which one walks,
finds the door shut,
and once again
gets caught, gets caught.

A captive heart,
a head, a hand,
an ear, the empty bed
is here—

A dull, an
unresponding man
or woman dead
to plan or plot.

Between what was
and what might be
still seems to be
a life.

HEAVEN

Wherever they've
gone they're
not here
anymore

and all
they stood
for is empty
also.

ECHOES

In which the moment
just left reappears or
seems as if present
again its fact intact—

In which a willing
suspension of disbelief
alters not only the judgment
but all else equally—

In which the time passes
vertically goes up and
up to a higher place a
plane of singular clarity—

In which these painfully small
endings shreds of emptying
presence sheddings of seeming
person can at last be admitted.

ECHO

It was never
simple to wait,
to sit quiet.

Was there still
another way round,
a distance to go —

as if an echo
hung in
the air before

one was heard,
before a word
had been said.

What was love
and where
and how did one get there.

ECHO

The return of things
round the great
looping bend in the road

where you remember
stood in mind
greyed encumbrances

patient dead dog
long lost love
till chair's rocking

became roar
sitting static
end of vision

day seems held up
by white hands were
looking for what was

gone couldn't come
back what was with
it wouldn't come looking.

ECHO

for Eck

Find your way out
no doubt
or in
again begin

Spaces wait
faced
in the dark
no waste

Were there
was here
was
always near

Sit down to see
be quiet be
friend
the end

VALENTINE
for Pen

Home's still heart
light in the window
all the familiar
tokens of patience

moved finally out
to let place be
real as it can be
people people

all as they are
and pasteboard red heart
sits there on table
inside the thump bump

passing thought
practical meat
slur and slurp
contracting lump

all for you
wanting a meaning
without you
it would stop

Coda

Roman Sketchbook

ROMAN SKETCHBOOK

AS

As you come and go
from a place you sense
the way it might seem
to one truly there as
these clearly determined persons
move on the complex spaces

and hurry to their obvious
or so seeming to you
destinations. "Home," you think,
"is a place still there for all,"
yet now you cannot
simply think it was

or can be the same. It
starts with a small
dislocating ache, the foot
had not been that problem,
but you move nonetheless
and cannot remember the word

for foot, *fuss, pied?* some
thing, a childhood pleasure
she said she could put her
foot in her mouth but
that way is the past again
someone's, the greying air

looks like evening here, the
traffic moves so densely,
you push close to the walls
of the buildings, the stinking
cars, bikes, people push by.
No fun in being one here,

you have to think. You must
have packed home in mind,
made it up, and yet all
people wait there, still patient
if distracted by what happens.
Out in the night the lights

go on, the shower has cleared the air.
You have a few steps more to the door.
You see it open as you come up, triggered
by its automatic mechanism, a greeting
of sorts, but no one would think of that.
You come in, you walk to the room.

IN THE CIRCLE

In the circle of an
increased limit all
abstracted felt event now

entered at increasing distance
ears hear faintly eye sees
the fading prospects and in-

telligence unable to get the
name back fails and posits
the blank. It largely moves

as a context, habit of being
here as *there* approaches, and
one pulls oneself in to prepare

for the anticipated slight shock—
boat bumping the dock, key
turning in lock, the ticking clock?

APOSTROPHE

Imaginal sharp distances we
push out from, confident
travelers, whose worlds are
specific to bodies—   Realms of
patient existence carried without
thought come to unexpected end
here where nothing waits.

HERE

Back a street is the sunken
pit of the erstwhile market
first century where the feral

cats now wait for something
to fall in and along the
far side is the place where

you get the bus, a broad
street divided by two
areas for standing with a

covered provision, etc. *Antichi!*
Zukofsky'd say—all of it
humbling age, the pitted, pitiful

busts someone's sprayed with blue
paint, the small streets laboring
with compacted traffic, the generous

dank stink floods the evening air
Where can we go we will not
return to? Each moment, somewhere.

READING/RUSSELL SAYS, "THERE IS NO RHINOCEROS IN THIS ROOM"

Wittgenstein's insistence to Russell's
equally asserted context of world as
experienced *things* was it's *propositions*
we live in and no "rhinoceros" can
proceed other than fact of what so states
it despite you look under tables or chairs
and open all thinking to prove there's
no rhinoceros here when you've
just brought it in on a plate
of proposed habituated *meaning*
by opening your mouth and out it pops.

ELEVEN AM

Passionate increase of particulars
failing passage to outside formulae
of permitted significance who cry
with foreign eyes out there the
world of all others sky and sun
sudden rain washes the window
air fresh breeze lifts the heavy
curtain to let the room out into
place the street again and people.

IN THE ROOMS

In the rooms of building James
had used in "Portrait
of a Lady" looking up to
see the frescoes and edging
of baroque seeming ornament
as down on the floor we are

still thinking amid the stacks
of old books and papers, racks,
piles, aisles of patient quiet
again in long, narrow,
pewlike seated halls for
talking sit and think of it.

HOW LONG

How long
to be here
wherever
it is —

I THINK

I think
the steps up
to the flat
parklike top

of hill by the Quirinale look
like where I'd walked when
last here had stopped
before I'd gone in

down to the Coliseum's
huge bulk
the massed rock
and the grassed plot

where the Christians fought
and traffic roars round
as if time
only were mind

or all this
was reminiscence
and what's real
is not.

ROOM

World's become shrunk to
square space high ceiling
box with washed green
sides and mirror the eye
faces to looks to see the
brown haired bent head
red shirt and moving pen
top has place still apparent
whatever else is or was.

OUTSIDE

That curious arrowed sound up
from plazalike street's below
window sun comes in through
small space in vast green drapes
opened for the air and sounds
as one small person's piercing cry.

WALK

Walk out now as if
to the commandment
go forth or is it
come forth   "Come out
with your hands up…"
acquiescent to each step.

WATCHING

Why didn't I call to the
two tense people passing us
sitting at edge of plaza
whom I knew and had reason
to greet but sat watching them
go by with intent nervous faces the
rain just starting as they
went on while I sat with another
friend under large provided umbrella
finishing dregs of the coffee, watching?

VILLA CELIMONTANA

As we walk past crumbling
walls friend's recalling his
first love an American
girl on tour who then
stays for three months in
Rome with him then off
for home and when he
finally gets himself to
New York two years or more
later they go out in
company with her friend
to some place on Broadway
where McCoy Tyner's playing
and now half-loaded comfortable
the friend asks, "What part of
yourself do you express
when you speak English?"
Still thinking of it and me now
as well with *lire* circling my head.

THE STREET

All the various
members of the Italian
Parliament walking
past my lunch!

AS WITH

As with all such
the prospect of ending
gathers now friends take
leave and the afternoon
moves toward the end
of the day. So too mind
moves forward to its place
in time and *now,* one
says, *and now—*

OBJECT

The expandable enveloping flat flesh
he pulls in to center in hotel
room's safety like taking in
the wash which had flapped
all day in the wind. *In,* he
measures his stomach, *in* like
manner his mind, *in*side his
persistent discretion, way, *un*-
opened to anything by *im*pression...

.   .   .

So often in such Romantic apprehension
he had wanted only to roam
but howsoever he weighed it or waited
whatsoever was "Rome" was home.

INDEX
of titles (in capitals) and first lines

299

303

ECHOES

Grateful acknowledgment is made to the editors and publishers of magazines in which some of the poems in this book first appeared: *American Poetry Review, Arshile, Beloit Poetry Journal, Bombay Gin, Die Young, Fishers, Gas, Grand Street, The Harvard Review, Lilt, lyric&, Michigan Quarterly Review, Notus, o•blēk, Poetry New York, Sagetrieb, Scarlet, :that:, Wallace Stevens Journal, West Coast Lines.*

Thanks too to the publishers of books and pamphlets in which many of the poems also appeared: *Alex Katz* (Marlborough, 1991), *Dutch Boy* (Living Batch Bookstore, 1993), *Gnomic Verses* (Zasterle Press, 1992), *Have a Heart* (Limberlost Press, 1990), *It* (Bischofberger, 1989), *The Old Days* (Ambrosia Press, 1991), *Parts,* with mezzotints by Susan Rothenberg (Limestone Press, 1994), *Raging Like a Fire: A Celebration of Irving Layton* (Vehicule Press, 1993), *The Scope of Words* (Peter Land, 1991), *WPFW89.3FM Poetry Anthology* (The Bunny and the Crocodile Press, 1992).

Thanks as well to Ken and Ann Mikolowski's Alternative Press for its printing of the postcard "Moral," to Elizabeth Robinson for the broadside "Death" and "Eyes," and to Ray DiPalma for the broadside "Here and Now" in the *Stele* series. Finally, a number of poems were prompted by a collaboration with the artist Cletus Johnson, among them those collected as *Gnomic Verses.* Exhibitions of these works were held at the Leo Castelli Gallery in New York, October 1990, and at the Nina Freudenheim Gallery in Buffalo, April 1991.

ACKNOWLEDGMENTS

MEMORY GARDENS

Grateful acknowledgment is made to the editors and publishers of magazines, chapbooks, broadsides, postcards, and anthologies in which many of the poems in this collection first appeared.

Magazines: *Columbia, Continental Drifter, Epoch, Slow Mountain, St. Mark's Poetry Project Newsletter.*

Chapbooks: *A Calendar* (The Toothpaste Press, 1983), *Four Poems* (Handmade Books, 1984), *Jim Dine: Five Themes* (Walker Art Center, Minneapolis, 1984), *Memories* (Pig Press, 1984).

Broadsides and postcards: "Bookcase" (The Folger Library, 1982), "Heavy" (Dancing Bear Productions, 1985), "Hotel Schrieder, Heidelberg" (The Toothpaste Press, 1983).

Anthologies: *Peace or Perish: A Crisis Anthology* (Poets for Peace, 1983), *In Celebration: Anemos,* Festschrift for Denise Levertov (Matrix Press, 1983).

The epigraph on the title page is quoted from Allen Ginsberg's *The Fall of America: Poems of These States 1965–1971,* Pocket Poets Series #30, copyright ©1972 by City Lights Books.

The epigraph on page 47 is quoted from Charles Olson's *Maximus Poems,* copyright ©1983 by the Regents of the University of California; used by permission of the University of California Press.

"Après Anders," the sequence on pages 42–44, is an improvisation on poems by Richard Anders found in his collection *Preussische zimmer* (1975).

WINDOWS

Grateful acknowledgment is made to the editors and publishers of magazines, newspapers, chapbooks, postcards, and anthologies in which many of the poems in this collection first appeared.

Magazines and newspapers: *A Dog's Nose, Arete, Black Mountain II Review, Blue Mesa Review, Bombay Gin, Boundary 2, Caliban, Conjunctions, Credences, Cutbank, Exquisite Corpse, Forbes, Giants Play Well in the Drizzle, Harvard Magazine, Human Means, Infolio, In Relation, Acts 10, Jerusalem Post, Literaturalmanach, manuskripte: Zeitschrift for Literatur, Napalm Health Spa, Notus, Nuori Voima, o•blēk, Organic Gardening, Painted Bride Quarterly, The Poetry Project, River Styx, Sagetrieb, Salt Lick Magazine, The Taos Review, Temblor, Western Humanities Review.*

Chapbooks: *The Company* (Burning Deck Press, 1988); *Dreams* (Periphery & The Salient Seedling Press, 1989); *7 & 6* (Hoshour Gallery, Albuquerque, 1988); *Window: Paintings by Martha Visser't Hooft, Poems by Robert Creeley* (The Poetry/Rare Book Collection, State University of New York at Buffalo, 1988).

Postcards: "Spring Light" (Limberlost Press, 1990).

Anthologies: *Poets for Life: Seventy-six Poets Respond to AIDS*, ed. Michael Klein (Crown, 1989); *The Green American Tradition*, ed. H. Daniel Peck (Louisiana State University Press. 1989); *Louis Zukofsky, or Whoever Someone Else Thought He Was: A Collection of Responses to the Work of Louis Zukofsky*, ed. Harry Gilonis (North and South, 1988).

Eight poems from the sequence "Eight Plus" were engraved on the bollards at Seventh and Figueroa, Los Angeles, dated July 20, 1988, by the Seventh Street Plaza Associates in cooperation with The Prudential Realty Group.

The epigraph for the section "Helsinki Window," from Malcolm Lowry's *Dark As the Grave Wherein My Friend Is Laid* (NAL, 1968) is reprinted by permission of Sterling Lord Literistic, Inc., copyright ©1968 by Margerie Bonner Lowry.